GROUP THERAPY
Who Needs It?

GROUP THERAPY
Who Needs It?

Doris Wild Helmering

Illustrated by Jan Boleto

CELESTIAL ARTS

Millbrae, California

To Skeeter, John, and Paul . . .
and
to Mom and Dad.

Copyright © 1976 by Celestial Arts
231 Adrian Road, Millbrae, California 94030

First Printing, September 1976
Made in the United States of America

Library of Congress Cataloging in Publication Data

Helmering, Doris Wild, 1942–
    Group therapy—who needs it?
    212 p.: ill. ; 22 cm.
    1. Group psychotherapy.   2. Consumer education.
I. Title.   [DNLM: 1. Psychotherapy, Group. WM430
H478g]
RC488.H47   616.8'.915   76-11364
ISBN 0-89087-159-0

1 2 3 4 5 6 7 — 81 80 79 78 77 76

CONTENTS

ACKNOWLEDGMENTS

Like all large undertakings, this book would never have been completed without the help of many of my colleagues, friends, and family. I would like to express a special "Thank You" to all who gave me hours of time and energy, reading, rereading, and making valuable suggestions in order that this book really shares with the reader what goes on in a therapy group.

Thanks to Germaine Eley for her valuable feedback for Chapters I and II and all the energy she gave sorting the material for Chapter IV. Thanks to Carla Cunningham for her many valuable suggestions throughout the text, particularly her suggestions about clearly tying the material together. Thanks to Elaine Kornblum for her help in clarifying a number of the TA concepts and for her creative suggestions with titles in the Table of Contents. Thanks to Kaye Stevenson and Judy Morris for their ideas and comments throughout the text. Thanks to Marty Groder and Ken Ernst for their helpful feedback regarding usage of TA terminology. Thanks to Carol Solomon and Fran Mues for their help in the fine tuning of the manuscript. Thanks to Rochelle Novack who did so much of the early typing and transcribing of tapes and to Tina Lampert who also spent hours transcribing material. Thanks, Kathy Hahn, for your transcribing, typing, retyping, proofing, and editing. You've all been great!!

There were many others who also made my writing of this book possible. Thanks to Judy Freiberg, who insisted that I get on with writing this book instead of going shopping. Many thanks to all my former teachers, especially Lillian Kaplan, who shared so much of herself with me. Also, thanks to Morris and Natalie Haimowitz who taught me a great deal while I was in training with them. And a very special thanks to all the people in all the groups who gave me permission to share the actual transcripts of their work in therapy.

While writing this book, my family also gave me encouragement and support. Thank you, Skeeter, for the many hours of good parenting you gave to our boys while I was busy with this book. And thanks John and Paul for just being.

INTRODUCTION

Group Therapy—Who Needs It? is a delightful and pragmatic portrayal of the actual process and events of Group Therapy. Transactional Analysis (T.A.), the primary method used is exceptionally well explained.

Doris Wild Helmering is an accomplished therapist whose education and background combine to effect a revealing and reassuring insight into the experience of Group Therapy. She received her bachelor of science degree in psychology in 1964 and her masters of social work degree in 1968 from St. Louis University, with advanced training in conjoint and family therapy at Purdue University and training in group therapy from Dr. Edgar Stuntz.

In private practice Doris has continued to train extensively with top therapists throughout the country. At present she has five ongoing T.A. treatment groups, supervises three T.A. training groups for therapists, serves as consultant for the Lutheran Family and Children's Services in St. Louis and is a field supervisor for students at George Warren Brown School of Social Services, Washington University. She has served as an instructor for the University of Missouri (Extension Division) and conducts T.A. workshops for government employees, persons involved in the helping professions and other interested persons. She received her Clinical Membership from the International Transactional Analysis Association in August, 1973 and is presently a Provisional Teaching Member of this organization.

Doris' book combines theory and therapy in a warm and human way. You will become familiar with the problems, successes and sometimes failures of people struggling with the basic and most difficult issues of change. No other book has given its readers such an on the spot, candid picture of therapy. The author's proficiency in cutting away the irrelevant and getting straight to the problem is illustrated within the taped sessions. An honest and aware worker in the field, she has also included and discusses her own misjudgments as a therapist. This is the first book of its kind available and I heartily recommend this work to professionals as an important adjunct to the basic books of T.A. theory. Even more exciting is the power of this book, as the title suggests, to fill the gap between fear and hope for Doris' group members or "fellow travelers" as she wisely prefers to call them.

Martin Groder, M.D.
Vice President, International
Transactional Analysis Association

PREFACE

Many people have all kinds of fantasies about what goes on in a therapy group. Charlie's therapist has just suggested that Charlie go into a group for treatment. Immediately, he begins to envision himself surrounded by all sorts of "crazy" people. If you have never been in a therapy group, perhaps your imagination would also run wild and you would fantasize a similar picture or worse.

There used to be an insurance company next to my office. When it was time for one of the therapy groups to begin, I noticed that the people working for the company would leave their door open. Often seven or eight workers would congregate at the entrance. Several group members started complaining about the stares they were getting from the insurance people. One woman remarked, "They act as though we have two heads." Although most of the group members expressed concern at one time or another about the stares they were receiving, one group member, Mike, did not seem to be particularly concerned. This made sense to me because he was a large, tough looking fellow with shoulder length hair and I figured that he elicited plenty of stares no matter where he went just because of his appearance. Also, he was a detective on the St. Louis police force and worked in some of the toughest neighborhoods. So, I reasoned that because of his job he didn't feel annoyed at the stares and rudeness of the insurance people.

One day as group time approached and the insurance people started to gather at their door, Mike arrived on the scene. As he was walking down the hall toward my office, he suddenly assumed the body posture of an ape and began screeching and jumping down the hall. At first there was silence—then came a giggle—then one by one the insurance people and the members of the group began to shake with laughter. After we all calmed down and wiped away our tears, Mike straightened up, grinned broadly, and introduced himself. From that day on the insurance people replaced their stares with smiles and nods as people came to my office for therapy. I think Mike's antics helped the insurance people recognize the absurdity of their fantasies and expectations about people who come for therapy.

Unfortunately, such fantasies and misconceptions about who comes to therapy are perpetuated and fanned by the media. Movies, television, and many national magazines dramatize and sensationalize what goes on in therapy groups. Either someone is planning, or has committed, homicide or suicide. Or, at the other extreme, everyone is "discovering the true meaning of life," by falling into each others arms and/or beds.

I am aware of the fantasies and distortions from both personal and professional experience. When I was a student in graduate school, part of my training to become a group therapist involved actual participation as a member of a therapy group for six months. Quite frankly, I was scared to death. Like Charlie, I feared I might be surrounded by "crazy" people or, even worse, that I might be crazy!

The first day I walked into the group with a smile on my face which was hiding my pounding heart and trembling knees. I quickly glanced around the room but recognized no one. I didn't even know who the leader of the group was. It was the custom of the school to assign students randomly to various groups in the area. It was ten minutes (or was it twenty hours?) before anyone in the group spoke. By this time, my anxiety level was so high that when the man sitting next to me spoke up, I jumped with fright. I can still hear his words, "What the hell are we doing here?" Several people tittered at his question. After a few minutes of everyone talking at once, someone finally asked, "Isn't there supposed to be a leader?" There was no response. As my thing is to be an organizer, I made the comment that I thought it would be a good idea if we all introduced ourselves and said why we were there. By the time eight of us introduced ourselves, the identity of the leader became known. When the leader introduced himself, he smiled. No one else smiled. I certainly didn't; I wanted to slug him for putting us through such unnecessary anxiety. I thought the group was for solving problems, not creating them!

By the third week three of the original eight had left the group. I remember asking the leader how and when the decision was made that these people would leave the group. Had they called and talked with the therapist personally? Did he tell them that they weren't good candidates for the group? How had it happened? He responded by saying, "You seem to have a lot of feelings about that, Doris." He never answered any of my questions. The only explanation we were ever given about the missing members was, "That's how some people respond to stress." As it would have been more stressful for me to drop the course than to sweat it out for six months, I stayed—but believe me, if I hadn't been a student, I would have run from that group. My guess is, the more healthy people in the group did exactly that!

Luckily, I had a friend, Jane, who was having a good group experience, and by our comparing notes, I realized that it wasn't group therapy that was the problem but rather the leader and his method of running the group that got my group almost nowhere. What I did learn from this experience was what I didn't want to be like as a therapist.

Although my first experience with group therapy was bad, I have had many good experiences since that time. I have also had the opportunity to train with many excellent group therapists and out of these experiences and my own thinking, I have developed a method of doing group therapy which I find both rewarding and successful for both fellow travelers (my name for patients) and myself.

The purpose of this book is to acquaint you with group therapy. Although the theory and therapy which appear on the following pages is based on my own personal value system and theoretical bias, I think it will give you a good idea of what group therapy is if you have never been in a group. If you are in a group or have been in a group, it will provide you with a basis for comparison. The one thing I regret is that much of the "feeling work" that I do in therapy is not part of this book. The printed word simply cannot capture the fear in a person's voice or convey the picture of a man crying in sadness.

Throughout the book are edited transcripts of therapy sessions. The names of therapists are the same. Those of our fellow travelers have been changed to protect their privacy. Each, however, gave me permission to share some part of their life with you.

In Chapter I, I have presented a transcript of a group which is meeting for the first time. This transcript will give you a realistic view of who comes to therapy and why. Chapter II presents various problems that people work on in group. In Chapter III you will see how small problems are often indicative of larger ones. Chapter IV gives a week by week account of three different people in group therapy. It is exciting to see the changes that these people were able to make in a short period of time. Chapter V looks at some of the ways people sabotage themselves so that they never solve their problems. Chapter VI talks about the myth that therapists are gods, and includes examples of how truly human we therapists are. Chapter VII gives information about who does therapy, how to go about selecting a therapist, and how I, myself, train therapists.

At one time or another in your life you have probably wished that you could be a little mouse in a corner. As a mouse you could see and hear what is going on behind the closed door of a conference room, or how your child is doing in school that day, or what Betty and Jim have to say about your new house. In reading this book you can be like a little mouse, but instead of hiding in the corner you can sit comfortably in an easy chair in front of the fireplace and find out what actually goes on in my therapy group.

I

NOW THAT YOU'RE
IN THE GROUP

Most people in therapy groups have much in common with you and me. People in therapy are of all ages, backgrounds, and ethnic groups. Some are well educated . . . some less educated. Some are rich and some are poor. Some are single and some are married.

Most fellow travelers who come for therapy have problems that are familiar. Some are parents struggling with raising their children, while others are children struggling to live with (or raise) their parents. Some are working on problems in their marriages, while others are making a decision to continue or end their marriage. Others are facing the problems that come with divorce. Some people come into therapy because their doctors have suggested that their headaches or chest pains are psychosomatic. Some are feeling depressed, some are having job problems or school problems, and some just don't know what is bothering them, but know they're not happy.

When working with people on their problems I use my own self, style, and personality plus various theories of human behavior. My basic theoretical framework is Transactional Analysis. I also use Gestalt Therapy, Behavior Modification, Reality Therapy, and Group Process. In addition, I place a strong emphasis on picking up on all behaviors which are in some way destructive. For example, if Sue continually interrupts in the

1

group, what she is actually saying is, "I'm more important than you are and I come first." This is not true and needs to be pointed out to Sue. However, when I do point the interruptions out, sometimes Sue will feel "put down," angry, and want to fight me. "How come she's so damn nit picky?" The reason "I'm so damn nit picky" is that people play out their life patterns over and over in small ways. If these patterns are confronted and not allowed to be played out, the person will learn a new, more effective way of relating and the larger destructive patterns which s(he) is following will also be discontinued.

A person who often interrupts in group believes that s(he) is the center of the world, or believes that being the center of the world is the only way to get what s(he) wants. Most people like to be center stage on and off throughout their life. If one person continually claims center stage, others don't have a chance at the starring role. Then what happens is that people wind up feeling angry with the center stage "hog" and eventually leave that person. So, Sue might be center stage but it's not going to be much fun when she doesn't have an audience!

My job is to help people learn how to get what they need or want in a healthy, nondestructive way. My style of therapy quickly helps people see their destructive behavior. What I know, however, is my style often evokes both scared and angry feelings. The person feels scared because s(he) realizes I will confront the destructive behavior no matter how seemingly insignificant the behavior is. S(he) feels angry because I am calling this destructive behavior to his/her attention—most people want to be seen as perfect. After the initial "shock" that they are not perfect and it is not "the other person's fault" that they are in such a mess with their lives, most people start to feel glad because of the behavior changes which result from the confrontations.

What follows is a transcript of a therapy group which was meeting for the first time. This group consisted of eight people, four men and four women.

They ranged in age from twenty-two to fifty-six. Each group member had seen Carla, the cotherapist, or me individually for two to five one-hour sessions. During the individual sessions specific problems were talked about and decisions were made about how these problems were going to be solved.

For example, one of the group members was Sharon, a twenty-eight-year-old divorcee who had come to therapy for a variety of reasons. She was having disciplinary problems with her twin boys. She was especially concerned about "screaming" at them. She was also unhappy with her job. Her main concern, however, was that she had trouble relating to men. Currently she was dating someone she really liked, but she was afraid to make a commitment because of her previous "get nowhere" relationships with men. Sharon and I had talked about ways she could go about solving these problems. The solutions to problems are referred to as goals. Sharon's goals were: get more information about the disciplining of her children; make some decisions about making her job better or looking at the possibilities of a new job; and check out whether Bob was the kind of person to whom she wanted to make a commitment. After her goals were decided, Sharon was ready to enter the group.

There are two possible ways a person joins a group. One is to enter a group that is just beginning. The other way is to come into an already existing group. Sharon entered a group that was meeting for the first time. None of the members had had previous group experience.

In a first group session my cotherapist and I provide a structure which gets people accustomed to our style of therapy right away. We give people positive attention when they behave appropriately and confront them when their behavior is inappropriate and could lead to problems for them. We also model by confronting and praising each other.

In order to make the transcripts easier to follow, all the therapists' names will appear in italics.

❖❖❖❖❖❖❖❖❖❖❖❖❖❖❖❖❖❖❖❖❖❖❖❖

THE FIRST GROUP SESSION

Carla—Hi. For those of you who haven't met me, I'm Carla. I am the cotherapist with Doris.

Doris—And I'm Doris for those of you who don't know me. Since this is everyone's first night in the group, we would like you to divide up into pairs. You will need to have a partner to do this exercise. The purpose of starting the group with an exercise is to acquaint each of you with the other group members, and also it will give us a chance to know you better.

When you get with the person you have chosen, I want you to face each other. Now what you're going to do is to become acquainted with the person you are facing. On the board is the information you are to find out about this person. You're to find out their name, occupation, marital status, why they came to group, what their goals are, how they feel about being here, and have them tell you three adjectives that they would use to describe themselves. Then what you're going to do is to come back into the group and introduce this other person and tell us these things about him or her and then give your impressions. We're going to give you fifteen minutes to get the information you need. Okay, any questions about the structure?

Group—No . . . no . . . none. [Group members talk to each other for the next fifteen minutes.]

Doris—Okay, first thing we want to do is to find out how you got together with the person you are going to introduce to the rest of us.

Mimi—I met Alice and we got together 'cause we happened to be sitting next to each other.

Doris—Who turned and made the initial move to get together?

Mimi—I asked Alice. Yes, I swung my chair around and asked her.

Doris—What I noticed was that all of you continued to sit after the instructions had been given, and most people just turned to the person closest to them.

NEIL—I did.

SHARON—Well, I'm scared, and it's easier to just swing my chair around than to stand up and go over to someone.

NEIL—Also, if someone else in the group had stood up and gone over to someone else, we would have done it.

Doris—Would you say, "If someone else had started it, I would have done it"? It's important that you speak for *yourself* and not other people. Why I am making an issue out of this is that often people get into games because they speak for other people, using the pronoun we, and do not take responsibility for themselves. For example, I don't like our dog, Fluffy, to prance around when we have company. But I often say, "I know you don't appreciate my dog sniffing around, so come on Fluffy, you have to go outside."

GROUP—[Laughter.]

NEIL—Yeah, I can see that. Okay, if someone had started it, I probably, I might, have done it.

Carla—Two discounts,[1] Neil. The words "probably" and "might." These words *qualify* your answer so we are really never quite sure where you stand with things. Do you understand that?

NEIL—Yes.

Carla—So would you say what you said again without discounting?

NEIL—If somebody else had done it, I would have done it.

Carla—Do you usually wait for someone to go first or to do something first?

NEIL—Yes, in this kind of situation.

JEFF—I started to get up, but people had already turned and faced each other, so I sat back down.

TODD—It was the line of least resistance.

Doris—What was the line of least resistance?

Todd—What's that again?

Doris—You said *it* was the line of least resistance, and what does the pronoun "it" refer to?

Todd—Well . . .ah . . .my behavior . . . what I did was that I just sat and waited for someone to start talking to me.

Doris—When in your life are you aware of taking the line of least resistance?

Todd—Quite often, I guess.

Carla—"I guess" is qualifying what you're saying, Todd.

Todd—Quite often I take the line of least resistance.

Angie—I wasn't able to make a decision, so when Ken turned to me, I smiled and we started talking.

Ken—Well, I asked Angie nonverbally. Like I just swung my chair around and looked at her.

Doris—I see, Ken. You didn't really ask Angie. Both of you got together, as if it "just happened" without taking responsibility for what *you* wanted.

Ken—Yes.

Angie—That did make it easier for me.

Doris—What happens is that people don't ask for what they want and consequently don't get it. It's like hoping for a birthday present without telling people that it's your birthday.

Group—[Laughter.]

Carla—Okay, let's get started with the introductions. You are to introduce your partner. What I don't want is for anyone to wait for Doris or me to ask you to introduce someone. We want you to take responsibility in this group from the start.

Ken—I'd like to introduce Angie, Angie Stone. Angie is a single girl, twenty-three years old. She teaches high school. She's involved with two men sexually and she has lots of goals. I can only remember a couple of them. Some of them are to get in touch with what she wants for herself and what she wants from people that she deals with. She feels some ambivalence about being in the group. And she described herself as . . . well . . . I've forgotten that.

Carla—What do you want to do about forgetting, Ken?

KEN—Ask her. Could you tell me again, Angie, what the adjectives were you used to describe yourself?

ANGIE—Yeah. Insecure, fearful, and scared.

Carla—Would you look at Angie and tell her your impression of her.

KEN—My impression of you is that you are very nice. I enjoyed talking with you and I was very comfortable with you.

Doris—I want to check something out, Ken. When you started out you were talking fairly loud, had good eye contact with the group, and then all of a sudden your voice got much lower and you stopped looking at people and started glancing at the ceiling, and I wonder what was happening? What were you saying to yourself?

KEN—"Oh my gosh, I've forgotten all that Angie told me." First, I tried to remember her name, and then I started to forget again and I felt foolish. Whenever I get myself in a situation where I need to meet new people, I'm always thinking that I'll mess up and forget their names. Like I'm really stupid!

Doris—I see. Now, you said you felt foolish. Would you change foolish to one of the four feelings that we use? *Mad, sad, glad,* or *scared?*[2]

KEN—Okay; I felt scared!

Doris—All right. Good. What I'd like to do now is explain some general TA concepts and then we can take a look at what Ken just said and see how that fits with the concepts. Eric Berne said that people have three ego states—Parent, Adult, and Child.[3] I'll start out by explaining the Child ego state. I will not be explaining it according to strict TA theory, but later on will refer you to some books.

When you first popped into the world, you brought with

you your Natural Child. The Natural Child is that part of you that is creative, spontaneous, fun loving, curious, and energetic. It also can feel sad, mad, glad, or scared. At about three months of age you start to develop what is referred to as the "Little Professor." This is your intuition. The function of the Little Professor is to psyche out other people. You are psyching out other people all the time, even though you may not be aware of it. In this group tonight, you have already used your Little Professor and psyched out who will do well in this group, who would be fun to go to lunch with, who will come through for you, give you what you want, and who will take advantage of you. It usually takes about a minute to psyche somebody out.

SHARON—You're kidding!

Doris—No. As an experiment, think about a relationship that didn't work out. What did you know about that person in the first five minutes of your meeting which was your cue that the relationship would not work out? . . . Okay, any more questions about the Little Professor?

NEIL—But men don't have intuition. So does that mean we don't have a Little Professor?

Doris—Both men and women have a Little Professor. However, men are taught not to use it as they are growing up. Instead they are taught and expected to be rational, logical, and unemotional; therefore, they are not to have a "feel" about something, whereas women are given *permission*, often *stroked*,[4] which means recognized, for their ability to intuitively figure things out. What Carla and I will be doing is giving the men in here permission and also stroking them for using their Little Professors.

ALICE—Why?

Doris—Because the Little Professor is a valuable part of your personality, the part which gives information at a preverbal level. Not using it is like not using all the fingers on your hand. In a family situation, the Little Professor figures out how to behave in order to get taken care of. For example, how will John Jones get his wants and needs met? In his family John's Little Professor quickly figures out that he must raise lots of hell, scream, and cry for at least twenty minutes in order to get mommy or daddy's attention. In the Kelly family Patty's Little Professor figures out that the best way to get taken care of is to lie very quietly and eventually mommy or daddy will give Patty the attention she wants.

When John continually yells and screams or Patty lies quietly to get mommy or daddy's attention, they are operating from their Adapted Child.

SHARON—Did you say Adapted Child?

Doris—Yes . . . the Adapted Child is that part of you which behaves in the ways the Little Professor has figured out for you to act in order to get what you want. The Adapted Child is also that part of you which responds to what mommy and daddy, or other significant figures in your life, tell you to do.

KEN—Will you give us some more examples of how a little kid adapts?

Doris—Okay. At age two and a half, most children adapt to family pressure and start using a potty chair instead of filling their diapers. At age four Michaeleen doesn't cross the busy street. She is in her Adapted Child. She really doesn't understand the possible consequences of crossing a busy street. She simply has adapted to what mommy told her.

SHARON—Well, I can see how when I'm having fun at the carnival that I'm in my Natural Child, and that when I get a "feel" about something it's my Little Professor working, but I'm not really sure how this Adapted Child concept fits in for me now that I'm an adult.

Doris—I can see how that's confusing. The fact is that people are always adapting, even as adults. In order to live we need to adapt to many situations. Stopping at a stoplight, standing in line, driving on the right hand side of the street, and dressing a certain way at work are all forms of adapting. We do these things largely without thinking about whether they make sense or not. The problem for many of us, however, is that we often adapt to what our parents told us or what the parent in our head tells us, rather than examining reality to see if the behavior makes sense. In TA we call this overadapting. There are two ways of overadapting. One is to be compliant and the other is to be rebellious. One such example was that when I was young I was told that "ladies do not wear pants." After examining reality, I discovered that many women I knew wore pants and were indeed ladies. So I stopped overadapting and following that parent message, "ladies do not wear pants," and replaced it with a new parent message, "ladies do wear pants." If I had not examined reality, but had started wearing pants as a way to "get Mom" this would have been my Rebellious Child. If I had continued to follow Mom's advice and never examined reality and never wore pants, I would have been operating out of my Compliant Child. One way to diagram the Child looks like this:

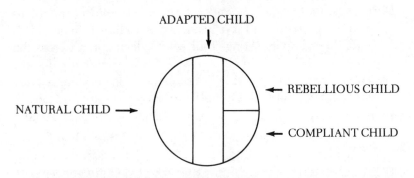

ADAPTED CHILD

NATURAL CHILD →

← REBELLIOUS CHILD

← COMPLIANT CHILD

JEFF—That diagram makes things more clear. But, what about the Little Professor?

Doris—Ah . . . the Little Professor is there. It's just that in TA we show him by using a different diagram. I think a good reference book is Berne's book, *What Do You Say After You Say Hello*. He has the various diagrams in there.

JEFF—Thanks.

MIMI—And what do you say after you say hello?

Doris—Why not!

GROUP—[Laughter.]

Doris—And now for the Adult . . . when we examine reality and make decisions based on this reality, we are using our Adult *ego state*. The Adult ego state is like a computer in that it takes in information and processes it. There are no feelings connected with the Adult ego state. For example, when you wake up in the morning, the man on the radio informs you that the streets are starting to ice up. Your Adult will process the information that you need to leave a half hour early in order to get to work on time.

Carla—So now we can add the Adult:

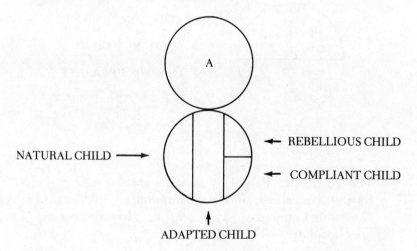

SHARON—Is it important for a person to always be in his Adult ego state?

Doris—No, but it is important to have your Adult ego state available at all times. I think when people initially started writing about the theory of TA, they indicated that the Adult ego state was the most important ego state and that people should always be in their Adult. Heaven help us if we were always in our Adult. How would you like to live in a society where everyone was like Mr. Spock in Star Trek?

GROUP—[Laughter.]

Doris—The Parent ego state contains all of the information you have been given from your parents and other significant parent figures. Your Parent ego state contains your value system and your prejudices. Often you can determine that a person is in her Parent ego state because she is expounding on the "shoulds" and "oughts" of behavior. I think it's helpful to divide the Parent ego state into four parts.

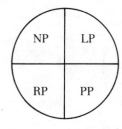

1. NURTURING PARENT

2. RESCUING PARENT

3. LEADERSHIP PARENT

4. PERSECUTING PARENT

The Nurturing Parent is compassionate, tender, comforting, concerned, and understanding. A mother in her Nurturing Parent may say to her son, "How about a cup of hot chocolate?"

The Rescuing Parent is one who is *overly* compassionate, tender, comforting, concerned, and understanding to the extent that the other person is allowed little or no independence. For example, instead of asking her son if he wants a cup of hot chocolate, a mother says, "What you need is a cup of hot chocolate." She is in the Rescuing Parent ego state and is discounting her son's ability to ask for a cup of hot chocolate or get himself one.

The Leadership Parent is one who makes judgments and uses authority in a good way. A father who says to his son, "Look both ways before you cross the street" is in the Leadership Parent position.

The Persecuting Parent is one who ridicules and is condescending with his criticism. A father who says to his son, "You're really stupid for not looking both ways before you cross the street" is in the Persecuting Parent position.

MIMI—From what I've read in TA, I thought it was a bad idea for a person to be in his Parent ego state unless he were nurturing.

Doris—On the contrary. Most of the beneficial rules and structures in our society are made and carried out from both our Leadership Parent and Adult ego states.

JEFF—Which ego state is it better to be in?

Doris—I think it depends. A person can respond to a situation from any ego state or he can respond from all ego states. For example, if somebody cuts you off on the highway, you will probably respond from your Parent, Adult, and Child.

You can respond from your Child ego state by giving him the finger, by cutting *him* off, by getting scared and getting off the highway, or by never driving again. You can respond from your Parent ego state by doing exactly what your mother or father would have done. For example, your Rescuing Parent might say, "Poor guy, must have had a bad morning." Your Leadership Parent might say, "Everyone should be required to take driving lessons." Your Persecuting Parent might say, "Damn fool." You would be responding from your Adult ego state if you processed whether to put your foot on the brake, move to another lane, or swerve to avoid a collision.

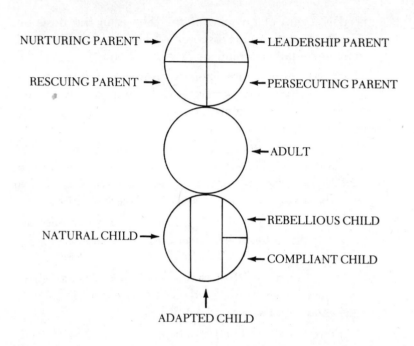

NURTURING PARENT →   ← LEADERSHIP PARENT

RESCUING PARENT →   ← PERSECUTING PARENT

← ADULT

← REBELLIOUS CHILD

NATURAL CHILD →   ← COMPLIANT CHILD

↑
ADAPTED CHILD

Most likely, you will move from one ego state to another very quickly in a situation like this. Your ego states will communicate with each other. This exchange between your ego states is called an *internal transaction*.[5] An internal transaction can be simple, involving only two ego states, or complex, involving all three ego states. Let's take the example I just talked about. A conversation with yourself may go something like this. The stimulus is the car cutting you off. You put your foot on the brake, Adapted Child, while your Natural Child says, "Give him the finger." Your Parent then says, "Don't give him the finger, it's not nice." Your Adult says, "I need to get my attention back to my driving."

MIMI—I have a question. What happens when two people relate to each other?

Doris—Then there are six possible ego states involved in transacting. I'll diagram what that looks like.

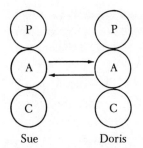

I ask Sue what time it is and she responds, "8:40." I have addressed her Adult ego state and she has responded with her Adult.

Sue   Doris

I tell you that I really like the shirt you're wearing, Neil. My Child is addressing your Child ego state. You grin and say, "Thanks" and your Child has responded to my Child.

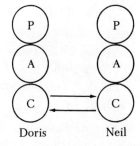

Doris   Neil

Does that answer your question, Mimi?

MIMI—Yes, thanks.

Doris—Now, using the information that I have just given, let's take a look at what happened with you a while ago, Ken. It sounds like the Persecuting Parent in your head was saying to your Child, "You can't remember; you're stupid." And your Child started to feel scared. I think you moved out of your Adult ego state and moved into your Child ego state where you felt scared and you wanted to get away. At that point, you stopped looking at people in the group and you left us. If we diagram what was happening, it would look like this:

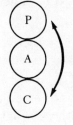

You can't remember; you're stupid.

I'm scared; I've got to get away.

KEN—You're right.

Doris—Okay, Ken, I want to check out one more thing. When

you were a kid, did anyone tell you either covertly (nonverbally) or overtly (verbally) that you were going to mess up? Perhaps someone said something like, "What's the matter with you, can't you remember anything?"

KEN—Some things to that effect. I can't remember any specific time, but when report cards came out, my folks always expected the worst. They always expected me to blow school, anything that had to do with academics.

Doris—Okay, you explained things really well in here until you started listening to the Persecuting Parent in your head. You don't need to listen to the messages in your head that say, "You'll mess up; you can't remember."

KEN—Right. I won't.

Carla—Also, your introduction of Angie was good, Ken.

KEN—Thank you.

SHARON—I'd like to introduce Neil, Neil Walsh. He's married, has four children, and he is a salesman. The main purpose for his being here tonight is to gain a better opinion of himself. He has just lost a very good job and is in the process of trying to find another one. It's a little difficult because of his age; he's fifty-six. He feels scared about being here, a little uneasy, but also happy that he's here. And we really didn't get adjectives about each other. I thought if I told you about Neil, you could figure out your own adjectives to describe him. So I didn't specifically ask for three adjectives.

Doris—Okay, did Neil volunteer three adjectives?

SHARON—No.

Doris—Was this a decision that both of you made, or did you, Sharon, say, "I don't think we need to do the three adjectives"?

SHARON—Well, I asked him for three adjectives, and then he said, "Oh, I didn't know that's what they wanted." Isn't that what you said, Neil?

NEIL—Right!!

SHARON—So we decided not to do it [said with a laugh].

NEIL—I did give you some adjectives about me, but I forgot to ask you about adjectives to describe yourself.

SHARON—You did tell me some adjectives?

NEIL—Yes.

SHARON—Oh, okay . . . [pause]. Well, Neil did say insecure, I think; I don't remember.

NEIL—Yeah, I said insecure.

SHARON—Okay, did you give me three?

NEIL—I probably did, but they are all synonyms.

Doris—Sharon, I'm going to tell you what I see you doing. You said, "We decided not to do it" and that sounded Adult. You also smiled, and that was your Child. I think your smile had a further implication which was to say, "So what are you going to do about it? Ha! Ha!" Let's look at this transactionally.

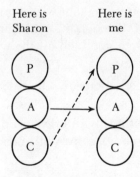

Here is Sharon   Here is me

Your Adult said to my Adult, "We decided not to do it," while your Child smiled and sent a *hidden message* to my Parent. All transactions which contain a hidden message are diagramed with broken lines and are referred to as *ulterior transactions.*[6] The hidden message was, "So what are you going to do about it? Ha! Ha!" When there is a hidden message, this is the first move, or *con,*[7] in a *game.*[8]

ANGIE—What is a game?

Doris—A game is a series of ulterior transactions which ultimately lead to bad feelings. Let's look at what happened with Sharon and see how what she said was a con for a game. On one level, the overt level, it looked as though Sharon was just giving me information about the decision not to get the adjectives. However, on another level, the covert level, Sharon was sending the message, "So what are you going to do about it?" Often when people receive two messages, an overt message and a covert message, they respond to the covert message and play a game. Had I not confronted Sharon's con, but instead bought the covert message, we would have been into a game.

SHARON—I see what I was doing. I did feel scared about giving three adjectives about myself. So it was easier not to do it than to worry about it.

Carla—What I also see you doing is making that decision for Neil.

SHARON—Probably so . . . right [laughter].

Doris—Okay. Everyone who is laughing or smiling with Sharon is giving her a message that it's okay to make decisions for other people. So I think the smiling is destructive. Sharon, can you think of any other reason that you wouldn't follow through with the assignment? You started out with a good introduction of Neil. You went through it bang-bang-bang. So is that what you do? Do a good job all the way through and then in the end mess up?

SHARON—I think it relates to how I feel about myself. I don't know.

Doris—Well, how about your relationships with other people? Do you start out having good relationships with people and then end up blowing it?

SHARON—I do have problems with relationships with people, but I think that's because I always pick a relationship that I know will never work out. And then, of course, it doesn't.

Doris—Well, does that mean you start out strong with someone and you do get involved, and then in the end you find out that it's no good?

SHARON—Yeah. I pick people who usually don't come through for me in the end. It's ridiculous, but that's what I do.

Doris—Okay, that's similar to what happened here; but this time it was *you* who didn't come through in the end.

SHARON—It's like a pattern then?

Doris—Um hmm. You made it through the exercise until the very last and then you didn't make it. You didn't come through.

SHARON—That would certainly explain school. Going through college for three-and-a-half years and not finishing.

Doris—Uh huh.

SHARON—Okay, so how do I change that about myself?

Carla—Let's start with tonight. What could you have done differently?

SHARON—Include the three adjectives.

Doris—And how could you do that right now?

SHARON—Well, Neil feels insecure about himself. I can't think of any of the other adjectives he used.

Doris—What can you do about that?

SHARON—Okay, Neil, what are the adjectives?

NEIL—Confused, insecure, and scared.

SHARON—That's right! Neil feels confused, insecure, and scared about being in the group.

Doris—Neat! You finished your job.

SHARON—So I have to realize that this is a pattern I have and I can break it by finishing absolutely everything I start.

Doris—Well, I don't want to go that far—that you *absolutely* have to finish everything you start. That would mean you have to be perfect. You can use your Adult to figure out what the important things are that need to be finished.

SHARON—Oh, so I decide what needs to be finished and what doesn't need to be finished. Okay, I understand.

MIMI—I'll go next. I'd like to introduce Alice Davis. Alice is a secretary, she's single, and she has come to the group because she has trouble dealing with people. She has trouble with her family. Um . . . she lacks self-confidence in

herself and she felt that by coming to the group and inter-
acting with the people here, it would help her deal with
people in other places. Her adjectives were nervous, insecure, and scared.

Carla—Oh . . . I forgot, I mean we didn't finish with Neil
because Sharon didn't tell Neil her impressions of him; and
you need to do that now.

SHARON—Oh, okay. My impressions of you, Neil, are that you
are very intelligent, and I'm glad that you're here. Your
goals are worth working on. You also seem like a sensitive
person.

Doris—I don't like what just happened. Mimi was introducing
Alice and all of a sudden you cut her off, Carla.

MIMI—I thought that maybe I had done something wrong.

Carla—You're right. I should have waited until you finished,
Mimi. I did cut you off and I apologize.

MIMI—Okay. I'll give my impressions of Alice. I feel that Alice
is very nice.

Doris—Tell her directly.

MIMI—Alice, you were very nice, very pleasant to talk to.
Somewhat shy and quiet, and very happy with your job. I
enjoyed visiting with you. You're a very good listener.

ALICE—Thank you.

JEFF—I'd like to introduce Todd Morris. Todd is married, has
five children, three girls and two boys, and he is an
engineer. And the reason why he came to the group was
that he felt bad about not being successful in his job or in
his marriage. Some of his goals are to feel better about
himself and his marriage. He feels scared about being
here, but also glad to have the opportunity to work on his
problems. The three adjectives he used to describe himself
were that he felt inadequate, hopeful, and encouraged.

Doris—And your impression of Todd?

JEFF—My impressions of you are that you are insecure and you
are nervous and scared.

Doris—Good introduction.

ALICE AND TODD—[Said at the same time.] I want to introduce . . .[laughter].

ALICE—Go ahead, Todd. You should follow because Jeff introduced you and now it's your turn.

TODD—Okay. This is Jeff. He's a bachelor and he is an accountant. He came into the group because he can't seem to find the right girl. He wants to figure out why while he's still young. He also gets depressed for long periods of time. He's nervous about being here, but nevertheless, he feels good about being here. The adjectives . . . [pause] I knew them a while ago. Um . . . did they slip your mind, too?

JEFF—The adjectives I used to describe myself are honest, open, and friendly.

TODD—My impressions are that you are honest, open, and friendly, and conscientious, and I think you're doing the right thing coming to the group.

JEFF—Thank you.

Doris—Okay, Todd, I think it's interesting how you shifted the responsibility of not remembering the adjectives onto Jeff. What you said was, "Umm, did they slip your mind, too?" And, Jeff, you didn't respond to Todd's question.

Let's look at what happened by using the Drama Triangle.[9] There are three positions on the Triangle: Rescuer, Victim, and Persecutor.

The Persecutor is into blaming others for his problems. He usually operates out of the position "I'm Okay, You're Not Okay."

The Rescuer is always trying to help someone, often at his own expense. He usually operates out of the position "I'm Okay, You're Not Okay."

The victim always looks like he needs someone to help him. His "come on" is a helpless, hopeless look. He usually operates out of the position "I'm Not Okay, You're Okay."

So, Todd, what you said to Jeff was, "Umm, did they slip your mind, too?" At that point, you sounded like a Victim, but I saw you in the Persecutor position of the Triangle because you were putting the responsibility for not remembering the adjectives onto Jeff. Then you became the Persecutor, Jeff, by not answering Todd's question. You then moved on the Triangle to the Rescuer position by giving Todd the adjectives. So I'm wondering if you often rescue others.

SHARON—That was really a good explanation, Doris.

Doris—Thanks, Sharon.

JEFF—Well, I do know that I always seem to get involved with girls who are on the rebound. And like I help them get through it. Make them feel okay about themselves and then they wind up leaving me for another guy. So you might say I rescue people who in the end persecute me.

Doris—*Might* say?

JEFF—I am a Rescuer and I end up being a Victim.

TODD—Did I persecute Jeff?

Doris—Did you?

TODD—Well, I guess I did.

Doris—Okay, I see you persecuting the whole group right now by asking me something that I already explained, and then fooling around with the issue. So let's go on. It's important that you don't get attention for persecuting.

Carla—I agree.

ALICE—I'd like to introduce Mimi. She has been married twice and has three children. She's a nurse. She came to learn how to better relate to her husband, her family, and her mom, who lives with them. She's scared about being here. She described herself as self-conscious, unhappy, and nervous. Her goals are to learn how to deal with anger and how to solve problems with her family. She seems very warm and very open.

Carla—Is this your impression?.

ALICE—Um hmm.

Carla—Tell her.

ALICE—You seem warm and sensitive.

MIMI—Thank you.

Doris—Good. I'd like to go back to you, Alice. What I noticed was that you immediately told Todd to go ahead, that it was his turn, when it hadn't been established when people were to come in. So, I'm wondering if that's something you do, give up your position to someone else.

ALICE—Yes, it is.

Doris—How did you feel about letting Todd go first?

ALICE—I felt good about it. Also, I didn't want to interrupt the mood that was going between Todd and Jeff.

Carla—What kind of mood was that?

ALICE—Well, the mood between them. Like things seemed to be going well for them.

Doris—Would you use another word for mood? Explain what you were feeling with one of the four feelings.

ALICE—Feelings? A feeling that I was getting?

Doris—Yes. What feeling, or feelings, were you having?

ALICE—Well, I was glad for them. And, this may sound strange, but a little sad for me.

Doris—Umm . . . well . . . I'd like to check something out about your past, Alice. Did you feel like your folks got together and you were left out?

ALICE—No.

Doris—How about your brother and sister?

ALICE—No.

Doris—Well, I'm thinking that something must have happened when two people were against you or you were left out.

ALICE—Well . . . my father and sister were and are very close and even today I still feel left out. In that respect, what you're saying is true.

Doris—Okay. I think what you experienced was a *rubber-band*.[10] A rubberband is a feeling from the past and a feeling in the present that snap together. So a certain event happens in the present which is similar to an event in the past and you reexperience the old feelings plus the new ones. I think your sad feelings were from the past because of feeling left out of the relationship with your father and sister. So when you saw Jeff and Todd together, you again felt left out. So both sads, sad for the past and sad for the present, were experienced.

ALICE—It sounds right to me; and what do you call it?

Doris—A rubberband feeling.

Carla—Yeah . . . I think Doris is right on.

MIMI—Oh . . . I just want to check out one thing. I notice that you ask people to put their feelings into one of four categories. I don't see why that's necessary or how that's even possible.

Doris—People use adjectives to describe the way they are feeling, and yet most adjectives about how one feels aren't clear. For example, if you, Mimi, say, "I'm feeling uncomfortable," Neil may think that you're scared. Alice may think that your chair is too hard, and I may think that you're angry. Because of this confusion with adjectives, what we ask people to do is describe how they are feeling with the words mad, sad, glad, or scared. Most adjectives to describe emotions can be broken into one of these four.

ANGIE—I don't see how that works. How about feeling guilty?

Doris—Guilty about what?

ANGIE—Well, guilty about having an affair.

Doris—My suspicions are that someone who is having an affair is *scared* that someone will find out and *mad* because of having to be careful.

GROUP—[Laughter.]

Doris—So if people use these four words to describe their feelings, all of us will have a clearer understanding of where people are. Also, there are different degrees or intensities to feelings. A person may be really angry or mildly irritated, have some sad or lots of sad. Why we want people to use four feelings is because people often discount feelings of low level intensity. Having to put the feeling in one of four categories helps people get in touch with their feelings better, whether the feeling is of low intensity or high intensity.

MIMI—Now I understand. I just think it will be hard to do.

Doris—Sometimes it is hard. I know for me it's hard, but often I can prevent myself from getting into a game if I know how I feel. If I can identify and admit my feelings to myself and/or others, then I can choose to do something with them or not to do something with them.

TODD—Why is that?

Doris—Well, our culture has set it up so that it's okay for men to feel angry and okay for men to feel glad. It's not okay for men to feel scared or sad.

KEN—I go along with that. I can remember my mom saying to me, "Boys don't cry."

TODD—Me, too. In fact, I rarely feel scared or sad.

Doris—My guess is that you do feel those feelings, but you don't recognize them.

TODD—Hmm . . .I'll think about that.

Doris—I know it sounds scary now, but it will get easier to express your feelings and you will understand better as we go along.

NEIL—Umm . . . Okay . . . I'd like to introduce Sharon King. She's divorced—a year and a half ago, and she has twin boys, age seven. She works part-time as a switchboard operator. She came into the group because she has trouble relating to men. Her past experience is that men aren't reliable. Presently she is dating someone whom she really likes, but she is scared to make a commitment because he, too, may not be reliable. That's one of her goals. She also doesn't express anger in an appropriate way. She does a slow burn and then pow—a big explosion! Another goal is that she wants to get more information about disciplining her children. She feels scared, but hopeful, about being here. I didn't ask her for adjectives because I thought I could deduce them.

Sharon, I think you have good feelings about yourself and you seem to have a good idea of what you're here for, and I think that's very good.

Doris—Okay, you didn't follow the instructions. You were told to ask the person to describe herself.

NEIL—Okay, I misunderstood. So I'll ask Sharon now. Would you give me three adjectives to describe yourself?

SHARON—Okay. Sensitive . . . scared, and uh . . . reliable.

Doris—Okay, good, Sharon. I'm wondering, Neil, if you often have information about something and then don't make use of it. I know from seeing you in individual sessions that it was very clear what you needed to do to keep your job, but you didn't use the information you had. You didn't do what you needed to do to keep your job, and consequently you were dismissed.

NEIL—That's right. That's something I will work on here.

Doris—Good.

❖❖❖❖

ANGIE—All right. I'd like to introduce Ken Wood. He's a student getting his Master's degree in business. Ken is single and entered the group so that he could learn how to handle his feelings and better handle other people's feelings. He made a point of saying that he wanted to learn how to handle his anger. He came to the group the day after he lost control and put his fist through the door of his apartment. Other times he has thrown furniture, and once he beat up his girl friend. That scared him so much that he decided to come into therapy. He is presently living with his girl friend, Betsy. Another thing he wants to work on in

therapy is to improve his relationship with Betsy. Three adjectives he used to describe himself are self-confident . . . well . . . uh . . . actually, we didn't discuss the adjectives. But I'll try to do the best I can.

Carla—Well, how can you follow the instructions?

ANGIE—I guess . . . uh . . . by asking Ken.

KEN—I think the adjectives would be insecure, scared, and angry.

ANGIE—Well, I guess one of the reasons I used self-confident as an adjective is because I had that impression of you. I admire your mind, your academic achievements, and you seem like an outgoing person. You're friendly and comfortable to be with.

Doris—Ken, I saw you rescue Angie. She fooled around with the adjectives and so you jumped in and told her without her taking responsibility and asking. I know that might sound picky, but Rescuers often turn into Victims, and that's what happened to you. You gave her the adjectives and then what Angie did was not use your adjectives. What she did do was to go back to the adjective she had decided upon.

So, Angie, you discounted Ken. The hidden message was, "My adjective is *better than* your adjective." So a game is played out. The game that you played out, Angie, is called NIGYSOB[11]; which, translates, "Now I've Got You, You S.O.B." Sometimes we refer to a NIGYSOB as a *kick*. I know part of the reason you're in the group is because you're having trouble with men. Kicking men is a great way to get them to leave you.

ANGIE—I see it, and I'm sorry, Ken.

Carla—Okay; has everyone introduced his or her partner?

GROUP—Yes . . . Yes.

Doris—Okay, everyone but us. This is Carla. She's a therapist, single, and is here because she likes to do groups. Her goals are to be a good group leader with people in here and to improve all the time. How she feels in here is a little scared about starting a new group. Also glad because it is exciting to do groups. Three adjectives she used to describe herself are growing, sensitive, and clever. My impression of you is that you are caring, creative, and fun to be with.

Carla—This is Doris. She's a therapist, married, and has two children, ages nine and seven. The reason she's here is that she likes doing groups. Her goals are to help people see what's going on, and also to help them change. She feels glad about being here. Also, she felt scared when we started as she didn't know all of you. Three adjectives she used to describe herself are caring, daring, and fun. My impression of you is that you're very bright, vivacious, and exciting to work and play with.

GROUP—[Laughter.]

Doris—All right, are there any questions or any feedback that people have before we go on?

GROUP—[All respond they are ready to go on.]

Carla—I'd like to say one more thing. During the introductions, some people were not looking at the person they were introducing, but instead they were looking at the floor. That is a way to discount yourself and others in the group.

KEN—I'm one of those people. Did you notice me doing that?

Carla—Yes, I did. But you weren't the only one, so I didn't want to make an issue of it just with you, Ken. Okay, I'm ready to move on. What we're going to do now is have everyone respond to how they felt about the group tonight and we're going to do it in a structured way. What I want everyone to say is, "One thing I liked about this group tonight is . . . and one thing that bothered me about this group tonight is . . ." In that way we know what you're thinking and feeling about the group.

TODD—One thing I liked about the group was that I didn't feel alone in my being scared because I think everyone else was just as apprehensive and unsure of the whole thing and . . . what was the other thing?

Carla—One thing that bothered me . . .

TODD—I'm trying to think of something. Hmm, that thing! The tape recorder. The thing that bothered me was that everything we said was being recorded.

JEFF—One thing I liked about the group was the way it was structured. I thought it was a lot easier than I anticipated. Another thing I liked was the way the two of you explained things tonight. TA makes more sense to me now. And one thing that bothered me was that I was so scared.

Carla—Do you feel less scared now than when we started?

JEFF—No . . . Well, yes, I feel *less* scared.

Doris—Okay.. It makes sense that you would feel scared in a new group. As times goes on you will feel less scared.

MIMI—I also liked the way the group was structured. It was a lot easier than I thought it was going to be. One thing that bothered me was that we were in this room for so long, and it took so long for us to get to know everyone else's name. And that's the way I felt.

ALICE—I liked the idea of the two of you being here. I think I'll get a lot of good feedback from both of you. And what bothered me was finding out that I feel jealous, well . . . I mean mad . . . and also sad about the close relationship that my father and sister have. Oh, one more thing I liked, and that was all the good information I got tonight.

NEIL—One thing I liked was that we started and that everyone is working hard and the thing that bothered me . . .

Carla—It's okay to look at us, Neil.

NEIL—The thing that bothered me was that we have to work so hard. In other words, you can't really relax because . . .

Doris—Would you say, "I" instead of "you"?

NEIL—I can't really relax because Doris and Carla are going to find something to make me not be able to relax about.

Doris—I'd like to respond to that. The kind of therapy that we do *is* scary for people in the beginning. We do pick up on lots of little things because we think that the little things really give us a clue to the bigger things people do. Like your not following through on the exercise, Neil. That's exactly what you do outside of here. You also didn't follow through with your job. Our picking up on that helps you see how you do that to yourself and then once you are aware of your behavior, you can change the pattern. Also, if we confront the kicks and digs and ask people to make clear statements, it will start to feel very safe in here. If we let things slip, it will be more scary for people and the trust level will drop instead of rise.

SHARON—I'd like to say that that is something I really liked about the group. When you did the comparison about my not stating the three adjectives with my not completing assignments, I saw my pattern immediately. I don't want to repeat the mistakes I've made and I don't want to come to this group and get nothing out of it. One thing that bothered me was that the group seemed very superficial. Like nobody has really gotten into any real problems. We have all said we are here and we have problems, and to one extent or another we are going to deal with them. But we haven't done anything, really!

JEFF—Yeah, it bothers me. I guess I was expecting to go into this "unbelievable thing" tonight and it just didn't happen.

GROUP—[Laughter.]

JEFF—It was safer that way, but I expected to get rid of at least ten problems.

GROUP—[Laughter.]

KEN—One thing that I liked about the group tonight was the way the introductions went and the way people opened up. Also, I liked all the information I got from both you, Carla, and you, Doris. One thing that bothered me was that there wasn't enough time.

Carla—Okay. Has everyone responded?

ANGIE—I haven't. I think a lot of people have said things about the group that I also think and I'm debating if I want to repeat what has already been said.

Carla—It's okay to repeat what someone has said.

ANGIE—Well, I think that everybody is searching for something, and I like that. It's like having a common goal. One thing that bothered me was that we didn't get to work on our specific problems.

Doris—That was good feedback, Angie, and you said it differently than anyone else. You don't need to discount yourself.

ANGIE—Yeah, thanks, Doris.

Doris—I would like to give feedback also. The thing I liked about the group was the clear way people presented their goals and the nonverbal support people were giving each other. People were smiling, nodding, and paying attention. The thing that bothered me was that I didn't know all of you in the beginning.

Carla—What I liked about the group is that the group seemed to start building a foundation of trust. I felt this by the way people interacted and the way people responded to information. What bothered me was my not knowing some people and not knowing what to expect from those people.

II

YOU THINK YOU'VE GOT PROBLEMS?

Problems are like jigsaw puzzles. Sometimes you lay all the pieces out . . . and voilá . . . there it is. You see the pieces clearly and how they fit together. The picture is complete. Other times you are so involved in hunting for a missing piece that you don't allow yourself to see the overall pattern which would help you complete the picture

Presented in the following pages are some of the problems which people have worked on in therapy group. The transcripts which you will read may be the culmination of many hours of work in therapy on a particular problem, or you may see a problem solved in a five-minute period of time.

The first transcript is about a woman, Betty, who is having problems with her mother-in-law. Betty thinks that if she is a good daughter-in-law she will be rewarded by having her children be good to her.

THE MOTHER-IN-LAW

BETTY—I'd like to work. It's about my mother-in-law. She demands a lot without really saying what she wants. I know what she wants. She wants me to volunteer to take her shopping. She doesn't drive, which makes it hard on all of us. But the hardest part is that she simply refuses to come right out and say, "Will you take me shopping?" So, I don't take her shopping because she hasn't asked, but then I feel guilty.

Doris—Using the four feelings, what do you feel when you feel guilty?

BETTY—Uh . . . well . . . a . . . mad!

Doris—Because?

BETTY—Because mother doesn't say what she wants.

Doris—She doesn't say what she wants. Um . . . sounds to me that two people are not saying what they want.

BETTY—[Laughter] You're right. Neither of us says what we want. I have never told her directly that I want her to tell me when she wants to go shopping. I guess I'm scared that she will ask me at a time when I don't want to take her. I'm also scared because I don't want my kids to treat me that way—the way I treat my mother-in-law.

Doris—Which is how?

BETTY—I know what my mother-in-law wants, but she won't tell me, and so I don't give her what she wants. I also refuse to ask her directly for what she wants.

Doris—And what's your fantasy if you don't tell your kids what you want?

BETTY—That they'll treat me the same way.

Doris—So how are you going to avoid that, Betty?

BETTY—[Laughter] Tell them what I want. Also, tell my mother-in-law what I want.

Doris—And then what are the possibilities?

BETTY—Well, my kids still have a choice to make. But I also might get what I want from them. They really are good kids.

Doris—Okay. Now what about your mother-in-law?

BETTY—Well, I'm going to ask her straight out what she wants to do. If she won't tell me what she wants to do, what I *know* she wants to do, I will go on and do what I want to do and not feel scared because I'm not being a good daughter-in-law . . . or mad because she is not telling me what she wants, or scared about how my children will act toward me, as I will handle things differently than my mother-in-law.

Doris—Good, Betty. I'd like to hear about what you did differently with your kids and mother-in-law next week.

BETTY—Okay [smiling].

❖❖❖❖❖❖❖❖❖❖❖❖❖❖❖❖❖❖❖❖❖❖❖

Now, not all people solve their problems so fast or have problems with their mothers-in-law. Some people have problems with their mothers. In this next section, you will see how Jenny lives with the belief that it is her job to make her mother happy, even at her own expense. Sound a little familiar?

HOLDING ON TO MOTHER'S APRON STRING

JENNY—I'd like to work. I hate rehashing things, but I haven't resolved the issue with my mother. So perhaps if I go over it again, I can get it resolved. I just came back from visiting her in New Orleans, and I'm feeling scared. I've had butterflies in my stomach all week. I haven't been able to organize myself, my thoughts are disorganized, and I feel that the butterflies are somehow related to my relationship with my mother. My husband and I had a really nice car trip to New Orleans. The first weekend was spent with my in-laws where we were pretty much on our own. We did what we wanted and enjoyed ourselves. When my husband left to come back to St. Louis, I decided that I had to spend some time with my parents, so I moved to their house. And from there on out, it was just a fiasco. Nothing specific except for the fact that as soon as I arrived at my parent's house my mother decided that I should call somebody to congratulate her because her granddaughter had just gotten engaged. I was very annoyed, mad, at the fact that Mother brought it up as soon as I walked in. I was mad that she was telling me what to do again. I was also mad at my reaction. What was I getting so upset about? Either I call, or I don't call. So what's all the hoopla about? The upshot was that things really coasted into a blowup with Mom on Friday. She kept nagging me and nagging me about calling this woman, until I finally relented and called her, but it just left me with a very bad feeling. I cannot have any contact with my mother, and not fall into this trap of first her telling me what to do, then my getting angry, and then finally doing what she wants, and then feeling more angry.

Doris—Come on. You don't just fall into a trap. You do get yourself in one, however.

JENNY—You're right. I'm still holding on to her apron strings. I guess it just boils down to the fact that I have to sever relations with her completely!

Elaine—Something I want to check out. Is that what you *want* to do, sever relations with her completely?

JENNY—No, but that seems to be the only way out. I can't even think of an option.

Doris—Well, let's talk about options. What did she say as you arrived in New Orleans?

JENNY—"Call up this woman and congratulate her, her granddaughter just got engaged."

Doris—What ego state was Mom in?

JENNY—Her Parent.

Doris—Okay, and which ego state of yours was Mom addressing?

JENNY—My Child.

Doris—And how did your Child feel?

JENNY—Angry! Very, very angry.

Doris—Okay, you felt angry, and then what did you do?

JENNY—I said, "No, I won't call her."

Doris—Did you tell her, "No, Mom, I won't call this woman!"

JENNY—I think so.

Doris—You *think* so, or you said, "*No*, I won't call her."

JENNY—I don't remember. I did tell her, though, that "I see no reason why I have to make calls for you. If you feel bad because I don't call this woman, it's your business." When I finally did relent and call, I said, "I'm only doing it because you're bothering me and I want to be left alone."

Doris—You didn't answer my question.

JENNY—Well, I didn't tell her "no" *directly*.

Doris—So you did what your Mom wanted, instead of what you wanted.

JENNY—Right.

Doris—So, if you do what somebody wants that is not what you want, what happens?

JENNY—Then I feel angry at myself and I feel angry with her.

Doris—And then what?

JENNY—And then I begin to lose confidence in myself.

Doris—What do you say to yourself?

JENNY—"You're stupid."

Doris—So then the Persecuting Parent in your head gets in on the act and says, "You're stupid." Then what?

JENNY—Then I start acting like a stupid child.

Doris—Okay, and then what happens with you and your Mom?

JENNY—Nothing. I'm angry with her and she's angry with me anyway. I ended up making the phone call and then and there she promised to leave me alone; but that night she started with another phone call she wanted me to make to a friend's daughter and I said, "If you say one more word, I'm walking out of this house."

Doris—Uh huh.

JENNY—But her nagging about making the second phone call didn't stop.

Doris—Okay, Jenny, how did you get yourself into this situation with your mother?

JENNY—How did I get myself into it? I don't know.

Doris—Oh, come on!

JENNY—By going there, by going to her house, by talking to her.

Doris—No, how did you get yourself into this situation?

JENNY—I could not tell her "no." She will not accept no.

Doris—Would you say, "I won't tell her no?"

JENNY—She will not accept "no." Even if I would have told her "no" the first time that she told me to call this woman, it would not have been the end of it. She actually stood in the middle of a party from the next table where I was sitting and said, "You've got to call this woman." I said, "Do you want me to pick myself up now and call her?" This went on every single time I saw her—it sounds absolutely crazy, but she will not accept "no." That is what I'm saying. The only option is not to discuss it, not to talk to her. There is no way of my saying "no" and her accepting it. You don't believe it. I can't help it, but that's the situation.

Doris—It sounds like your Adult was not in on the act. First you were the Overadaptive Rebellious Child, "I'm not going to do it." Then an Overadaptive Compliant Child, "All right, I'll do it and I'll get you off my back."

Elaine—So what would be different this time?

JENNY—I'd stay away. That's what I'm saying. I have to walk out and stay out.

Elaine—Well, I'm inclined to agree with you on a temporary basis. You allow your mother to win every time, so she has the information that you rebel and get mad and do all kinds of stuff, and then in the end you do what she wants.

JENNY—Okay, all right! [Said angrily].

Elaine—Hmm . . . What did you hear me say to you?

JENNY—That in the end my mother always wins and that's why she will not take "no" for an answer. Until I learn to say "no" and mean it, she will continue to insist on me doing things.

Elaine—That's right.

JENNY—All right, last year we had an episode when she came into town to visit us.

Doris—Wait a minute. I think you're not going to use the information you have because what you're saying is, "Now let me tell you another story."

JENNY—But it's not another story, in a way.

Elaine—Let's see if you agree with me or not about what I said to you.

JENNY—Yes, I agree, *except* for the fact that I don't see that there has to be a severance in the relationship.

Doris—Hold on. It was your idea that the relationship had to be severed.

Elaine—Sounds like a fancy "Yes, But"[12] . . . I give you information and you say, "Yes, but . . . I can't do it that

way." So I give you more information and you say, "Yes,
but that won't work." So I give you more information and
again a "Yes, but that won't work either." So you're getting lots of attention for arguing with me and Doris. In the
end, you will be able to prove out that we, Parents, are not
okay because we couldn't help you solve the problem. So
I'm not sure if you are really interested in solving this
problem with your mother, or if you are simply interested
in proving that the group, Doris, and I can't help you.

JENNY—You're right. What I need to do is to stop relating to my
mother until I can say "no" to her and mean "no." So I'll
need to tell her that I'm not coming to her house for
Thanksgiving. But I'm scared to do that because I'm going
to hurt her. I'm afraid to hurt her; I feel guilty about it.

Elaine—Now you're "yes-butting" yourself. Also, what Doris
said is right. You believe that you are responsible for how
your mother feels. You believe her happiness in life
depends on you.

JENNY—Well, there is no doubt that I'm going to hurt her feelings by telling her that I'm not coming, whether or not she
depends on me for a reason to live.

Elaine—It might hurt; it will not kill her. It might be the first
step in a real relationship. Right now it's like an operation.

JENNY—It sure is.

Elaine—It doesn't mean that you will never relate again. It only
means until things change.

JENNY—I keep thinking that there must be something wrong
with me if I can't get along with my mother. What kind of
person am I?

Doris—What kind of person are you?

JENNY—I'm a daughter who would like to improve her relationship with her mother—who basically loves her mother and
wants to have a good relationship with her.

Doris—Keep going.

JENNY—And who has never been able to do it, and who doesn't

want to hurt her mother, but who ends up hurting her anyway, regardless.

Doris—What else does this daughter want?

JENNY—To be happy and to help her mother to be happy, if that is possible.

Doris—Your mother has set it up so that one of you has to be dependent upon the other. One of you wins and the other loses.

JENNY—Right.

Doris—And if your mother wins, you won't grow up. which is what your mother *wants*, *not* what your mother *needs*. It may also be what you want, but not what you *need*.

JENNY—I guess that's what I want. I want to please her and also make my own decisions. I want to be grown-up but also do what she says. It is impossible!

Doris—Uh huh.

JENNY—Okay, I'm finished working for now.

Jenny continued to work on this problem and eventually made a decision to let go of her mother's apron string. Her mother wanted her to come to New Orleans for Thanksgiving and Jenny wanted to stay in St. Louis. There were several tearful phone calls from Mom who was subtly and not so subtly saying, "How can you do this to me after all I've done for you?" The final plea came from Jenny's father who called his daughter and told her how miserable she was making her mother. Despite the pressure, Jenny did not go to New Orleans, and she let go of the apron string. At Easter Jenny visited her mother and found that she was indeed grown-up. She could say "no" to Mom, and still know that both she and Mom were okay.

❖❖❖❖❖❖❖❖❖❖❖❖❖❖❖❖❖❖❖❖❖❖❖❖❖

If you are a parent, you will probably find the next section very interesting. My ability to help parents solve problems with their children came from many sources. First, I read almost anything I could get my hands on about child rearing. Unfortunately, many theories are contradictory and I found them to be of little value in helping parents deal with problems that they were presently having with their kids. What I finally concluded was that unless we could take our kids back to their day of birth and start all over, there were few answers in these books. Second, since I am also a parent, I was experiencing some headaches with my own children. My husband and I were spending a great deal of time in discussions about "what to do" and "the best way to do it" with the boys. After much thought and discussion, as well as trial and error, I developed an effective method for working with parents and with children based on Rudolf Dreikur's theory of Natural Consequences. Since I have been using the method which I call "Positive Stroking, Plus Consequences for Irresponsible Behavior" my own life and that of many of my fellow travelers and friends has greatly improved. The stresses and strains of parenting don't seem stressful and strainful any longer.

The theory is really quite simple. Children need a great deal of love and affection. They need to be stroked for just being alive. "I love you, Patty. You're such a wonderful little girl." Transactional Analysis calls this form of recognition giving Patty a positive unconditional stroke. That means that Patty doesn't need to do anything or say anything for the stroke. She is just stroked for being alive.

The second kind of recognition a child needs is called positive conditional stroking. "That is a fine picture you drew, Mike!" Thus, Mike was stroked for the picture that he had drawn.

In addition to positive strokes, kids also need to have a good structure. You know yourself that if you are aware of how you are to dress for a certain dinner party, you feel safer. Or if you know what the boss expects, you will be able to evaluate your own preformance and also will do a better job. So, too, with children.

Now, many times parents tell their children what they want. "I want your bed made in the morning, your room cleaned, and your toys picked up." They also spell out that there will be no belching at the table, no bad report cards, and no interrupting when Dad or Mom is on the phone. When kids get older and are teenagers, parents expect them to talk courteously, to greet others with an audible "Hi" instead of a "caveman grunt", to take a shower a day; to wear a "reasonable" hairstyle, and observe certain curfews during the week and on the weekend.

Often these expectations are spelled out over and over . . . louder and louder . . . but many times there are simply no real consequences for the children not meeting these minimal expectations.

I myself used to rant and rave at my son, John. "If you really loved me, you would care about me and do well in school." Or to my other son, Paul, I would say, "If you care about my feelings, you will put your clothes in the hamper after your bath, instead of leaving them lay all over the floor." Well, I do think John and Paul love me, and do care about me and my feelings . . . but not as much as I want them to care. I also know that my husband and I *care more* about their school work and the messy bathroom floor than they care. The bane of all parents!!

The solution to our solving these problems came when we decided to stop concentrating on how much *we* care and figure out what our *kids* care about and use that information as leverage. My husband and I knew that John, age nine, cared very much for soccer, his soccer ball, playing outside, desserts, and television on Friday night. Aha! The light dawned! "John, if you do not complete your math homework, you will not play soccer on Saturday." Well, John made every game this past season and he also completed his math homework. One night at the dinner table he had this to say, "You know, Dad and Mom, I don't care a darn about school, but I sure care about soccer."

Paul, two years younger, cared about television, friends coming to the house, his roller skates, and his record player. Paul did not come home one night after school. After several telephone calls my husband located him and informed him to "get his fanny home." When he came into the house with a guilty look on his face, we didn't wring our hands, go into a typical parent lecture, or spank him. What my husband did say was, "No television Saturday morning." Paul and John now know that there is a consequence for any irresponsible behavior. Is this method effective? Yes!! Is it hard to enforce? Sometimes.

I think in our culture we as parents are overly concerned with showing that we love our kids and wanting our kids to love us. As a result we often are very scared to discipline our children because we fear their withdrawal of love and affection. My husband and I want our kids to think well of us when they grow up, but not at the expense of our comfort nor at the expense of their need for guidance during the years of their growing up.

As the children get older, we expect that they will continue to see how far they can push us to get their own way. They may be angry, perhaps even threaten to leave home if we don't go along with their plans or desires. They may compare us unfavorably with their friends' parents. They will probably try to figure out ways to test us in regard to our values and our exceptations as parents. An example of such testing would be we tell them to have the car home by 10:30 P.M. and they come in at 10:50 P.M. Now there will be a consequence for these twenty minutes so that they will bear the responsibility for their actions.

You will understand what I mean when you read the following transcript where Betty talks about the problem she is having with her teenage daughter, Marsha.

ADOLESCENCE—I'LL NEVER GET THROUGH IT

BETTY—I want to work. I'm having some real problems with Marsha, my fifteen-year-old. She is not sharing household responsibilities. Also, I'm concerned about her room. I know that I can always close the door to the room if it's a mess, but there are some things I can't just close the door on. Like chips in the furniture, opened bottles of make-up and perfume left on her dresser. Potato chips mashed in the carpet. Also, coke spilled on the carpet and some of these stains are just not coming out. It's okay if she wants to leave the bed unmade and doesn't pick up her clothes and so forth, that's fine! It's her room. But I am concerned about the things that we're going to have to replace.

Doris—Hold on; are you sure it's fine that she doesn't pick up her clothes or make her bed?

BETTY—Well, I was told by her counselor at school that her room is *her* domain.

Doris—Okay. But that's not my question. Are *you* concerned about her room?

BETTY—Yes, I'm concerned about her room!! It's a terrible mess!! It gets messier every day.

Doris—So she's persecuting you with her messy room.

BETTY—Yeah, right! And she's getting to me. I close the door of her room, but then I open the door. [Laughter].

GROUP—[Laughter.]

BETTY—Another thing, you know, clothes cost a lot of money, and where do Marsha's clothes land? They land on the floor where they're stepped on. We also have an agreement. She's asked to borrow some of my things and that's fine with me, *if* she takes care of them; but she doesn't.

Doris—And you keep lending her your clothes?

BETTY—I confess! [Laughter.] When I get real angry, I say, "You can't wear my clothes any more because you're not taking care of them." Then we have three or four sweet days, and I say, "Yeah, you can wear my blouse or slacks." You know, I really don't want to lend her my clothes.

Doris—So where are you on the triangle when you allow her to borrow your clothes?

BETTY—I'm a Rescuer. I don't want to lend her my clothes, but I do it anyway. I discount myself, but I think if I say "no" then I'm the Persecutor.

Doris—Are you persecuting?

BETTY—No! Marsha might think I'm persecuting if I say "no," but that's an okay decision for me to make.

Doris—So how can you get yourself off of the triangle?

BETTY—I can get myself off of the triangle by not lending her clothes. Then there won't be any problem. I just don't want to lend my clothes.

Doris—Well, shouldn't mothers lend clothes to their kids?

BETTY—Only if they want to.

Doris—Would you say that stronger?

BETTY—Yes. It's okay that I choose not to lend Marsha my clothes.

PAUL—I think not lending her your clothes sounds like a good solution.

BETTY—Another thing. Right now she's very moody. I'll come home and be in a happy mood. I go knock on her door and I want to tell her about something exciting or ask her a question, and she just lashes out at me. I just don't know what to do at that point. Do I ignore her behavior or fight her or what?

Elaine—Well, what have you done in the past?

BETTY—I've done both. I've fought and also I've ignored it.

Doris—And what has been most effective?

BETTY—Neither. I guess I need to tell her that I'm angry and I won't tolerate such behavior.

Elaine—Are you going to do that?

BETTY—Yes, I'm going to stop letting her shit on me.

Elaine—And how are you going to stop her from shitting on you?

BETTY—Well, make her share in the responsibility of keeping the house clean. When she takes food into the den, she will have to put it away, she will have to clean up after herself. If she doesn't come through, then I'll have to get a little bit stronger.

Elaine—How?

BETTY—Gee, this is tough for me! Well, I'll have to take something away.

Elaine—What?

BETTY—Something that's really important to her. Let's see, what would be really important to Marsha? Okay, her driving lessons, the telephone—that would get her! [Laughter.] You know, I took the damn phone away several times and then gave it back to her. I put the phone in my car trunk and brought it back out after several weeks when the relationship improved. That bothers me, too.

Elaine—Why?

BETTY—Because I gave the phone back. And then we got back into the same things again. She started shitting on me and the whole family again.

Doris—Then what did you do?

BETTY—I allowed her to continue to use the telephone. I guess I'm not so smart.

Doris—So what do you need to do next time?

BETTY—To make it very clear to Marsha that if I remove the phone, she will need to start improving her behavior before she gets the phone back. And once she gets it back she will continue to behave like a human being instead of some creature from Lower Slobovia. And, if she doesn't . . . out goes the phone!

You know, I think she really wants to get me. She knows I'm bothered by her room. Why does she want to get me?

Doris—The reason Marsha wants to "get you" is because you are a parent, and in control.

Elaine—AMEN!! Teenagers think that they are grown-up, and so just walking in the house and looking at their parents who are still in control of them makes them furious. It's a double bind for teenagers. They are supposed to be grown-up, but at the same time, still are dependent on their parents.

BETTY—I think you're right. Okay, so what I'd like to say to her tonight is that beginning tomorrow I'd like her room cleaned. And, if it isn't cleaned, I'm going to remove the telephone and it will stay removed until I see that for ten days the room is cleaned.

Doris—Fine. Now then, suppose after ten days you give her back the phone, and the next day the room is a mess again.

BETTY—The phone goes out—a stronger out.

Doris—What does that mean?

BETTY—It means that the room will have to stay clean for a longer period of time. This time it will have to be clean for twenty days before she gets the phone back.

Doris—Hurrah for you!!

GROUP—[Laughter.]

BETTY—And if she continues to press me . . . well, the third time around I remove the phone permanently. We really don't need two phones; it's a luxury we can do without!

Doris—Now you're being a strong parent! Something you need to be for your own protection and something Marsha needs for her own safety.

❖❖❖❖❖❖❖❖❖❖❖❖❖❖❖❖❖❖❖❖❖❖❖❖

It is typical that many people, perhaps even you, start to feel bad because something changes or goes wrong. Your husband comes home and announces that he has been transferred, and you will need to pack up and move some two thousand miles away in the next six weeks. Or, just when your son is finally starting to adjust, settle down and do well in school, his teacher announces that she is pregnant and will not be able to teach the rest of the term. Or your babysitter, who is a real gem, tells you on Wednesday that Friday will be her last day.

There is an alternative to letting an incident like this throw you, because it is *you* who determines how you will act and feel with each and every event that takes place in your life. *You decide* how many minutes, or days, will be spent thinking about some disappointment or failure in your life. *You* also decide when you will stop feeling bad and start feeling good.

In the next transcripts, Karen in the first, and Jack in the second, both decide in very concrete ways what they will do to change how they are feeling.

THE ONE THAT GETS LEFT BEHIND

KAREN—I'll work. Last week I was feeling jealous . . . well, mad, because Sue, a close friend of mine, got married. I was also feeling really lousy because of all the time she was now spending with her husband instead of me. So last week I made a contract to get in touch with some of the consequences of feeling like a Victim and continuing to rehash how it used to be with Sue. So, I did that. What I came up with is if I only think about Sue, I will not allow myself to make new friends. I will continue to be dependent on Sue and never get close to anyone else. If I hold on to Sue, I also won't have any time to develop a relationship with a man. So . . . after I thought about it, I called up someone at St. Michael's Church to find out about the Graduate Club. I thought maybe I could meet other people there. [Smiling].

There is one more thing I want to add. I saw Sue on Wednesday, and we discussed the summer program about remedial reading and math we are doing together. I didn't act like I was hurt. I acted silly, I acted glad. I was fun. I now know I can go on with my life. My happiness doesn't depend on Sue, and I can keep her as my friend.

Doris—I think that's really neat the way you chose to give up being a Victim and make a new decision about your life. Also, it was really good the way you took home the information that you got last week and used it this week.

MICHAEL—That's really great!

KAREN—I think it's great, too!

GROUP—[Applause and laughter.]

THE MAKING OF A PIZZA

JACK—I want to work. I want to talk about the trip I took last week because it was really a big event. Dick, my friend, and I went to stay at his folk's cottage in Wisconsin. We spent five days there and it was the first time I have really felt free since I graduated from dental school. I was responsible for nobody but me. I did what I wanted for a week. I got really high just playing the guitar and reading and doing exactly what I wanted to do. I even got in some fishing. I was happy the whole time. Everything just sort of came together. As soon as I came home, things changed. Shari wasn't there. She had to go out of town on a two day business trip which meant that I had to come home to an empty house. I felt scared and angry that she wasn't there.

PETER—Did you know in advance that she would be gone?

JACK—Yeah, I called her right before I came home and found out that she had to go out of town on business. I understood in my Adult, but I felt upset about it the next morning. I curled up in bed like a little puppy, and I just sort of started whimpering, and finally I realized that I wanted Shari to take care of me. I wanted somebody to take care of me! I didn't want to take care of myself. And then I started laughing and I realized that I didn't have to feel sad and helpless and that what I wanted to do was to take care of myself. After all, I'm a grown man of 29. After making this decision, I had a really good day! I got out of bed and prepared a big pizza for the two of us. And when Shari came home, I had it ready. We had a neat evening together, and I know that I made it happen.

PETER—You did a really good job, Jack getting yourself out of your own misery.

GROUP—[Strokes Jack for doing good work for himself.]

❖❖❖❖❖❖❖❖❖❖❖❖❖❖❖❖❖❖❖❖❖❖❖❖

When you were a little tyke, just about one foot high, your Mom or Dad probably made a great fuss over your first words. Later they cheered you as you waddled unsteadily across the room for the first time. When you got older, and could tie your own shoes, you received a proud smile for your accomplishment. As the years passed, you learned to do many things for yourself because of one big word—permission. Your parents gave you permission to think, permission to ask questions, permission to be curious, and permission to figure out options and solve problems.

Some people do not get this permission. They were told they were stupid; people frowned when they were curious or asked questions; or someone was always solving their problems for them so that they never learned how to solve their own problems.

I personally think that permission is one of the most valuable concepts in therapy. By permission I mean that the therapist and/or the group gives a person the go-ahead to do something different than s(he) learned as a child. A person may get permission to live and enjoy life, or permission to think and solve problems, or permission to stop being a Victim in life, or permission to get taken care of.

If Mimi has been told all her life by well-meaning parents that when little girls grow up they should get married and raise a family, Mimi will need permission to do something different with her life. In therapy, Mimi can get permission to use her brains and go into business for herself. She can also get permission not to follow her parents advice and have to get married, or she can get married and have a career. In other words, she now has a choice.

If Joe has been told all his life that he is just like Uncle Mac, who is a cheating scoundrel, Joe can get permission in therapy to live out his life in a different way.

In the next section, you will see how clever Louise is after receiving permission to solve her own problem.

THE DECISION

LOUISE—I would like to work.

Doris—Fine.

LOUISE—I have to decide if I'm going to school this summer. My doctor says I need more rest and he advised me not to go to school this summer, but I want to. And yet, I think it might be too much for my health . . . but then, I start thinking about how stupid I'll be if I don't go to school this summer; that I won't have all this knowledge.

LAURIE—You mean you won't have your degree as quickly. That's what I hear you saying.

LOUISE—Right. Because I have to pay tuition within the next ten days, I need to get this resolved tonight.

Doris—So what do you want from the group, Louise?

LOUISE—I don't want you to tell me what to do. I just want to talk about it and decide for myself.

Doris—Okay. Suppose you be your own therapist. Put a chair in front of you and run the problem out for your therapist.

LOUISE—Okay, I'm me first. [Louise settles back in her chair and talks to the empty chair in front of her.]

I need to decide if I'm going to school this summer. Or, I could take the summer off and start again in the fall, but if I do that, I keep telling myself that I'll be stupid for the summer because I will not be using my brain.

LOUISE—[As therapist—switches chairs.] Is it true that you will be stupid if you don't go to school this summer?

LOUISE—[Switches chairs.] It is not true that I'm stupid. Also, I'm afraid that if I go on with this conversation, I will be yes-butting.

LOUISE—[As therapist—switches chairs.] So don't do a "Yes-

But," but do go on and get this issue solved. Tell me, what are your alternatives, Louise?

LOUISE—[Switches chairs.] I could take the summer off and start in the fall, and I could do a lot of reading this summer on my own. I don't know where to go from here.

LOUISE—[As therapist—switches chairs.] Would that be helpful if you did reading on your own and didn't go to summer school?

LOUISE—[Switches chairs.] Yes, it would. I'm going to get the names of some books that pertain to my field of interest and read them this summer and then start back to school in the fall. I've solved the problem.

Doris—You are a good therapist.

GROUP—[Laughter.]

LAURIE—That sounds neat, and it only took you five minutes to work that out.

Doris—You did a fine job, Louise.

VICKY—I like the way you think.

BEVERLY—I think that was clever the way you worked that out and got the problem solved.

LOUISE—Thank you, everybody.

THE GRADUATES

The above examples show that people can and do work through a variety of problems in group. In case you're wondering if anybody ever gets out of a group once they're in one, the answer is a loud "YES!!!" Some people are in group for several months, whereas others stay in a group for a couple of years. I would say that the average time spent in my therapy groups is about sixteen months. I know that sounds like a long time when you think about it. But then, that's about how long two winter bowling leagues last!

When someone accomplishes his/her goals in therapy and the group and therapist agree that the goals have been achieved, the person is ready to graduate, or leave group. In our groups we have set a structure that a person must announce that s(he) is ready to leave group one week prior to their actual leaving. The week a person announces s(he) is ready to leave, the group members and the therapist give him/her feedback as to how they think and feel about it. If the feedback is generally positive, the following week we have a graduation party. In the next three transcripts you can see how this process actually happens. Ellen, Pat, and Ronnie were all in different therapy groups and all were ready to graduate.

Ellen was in therapy about ten months. She had consistently worked hard and her confidence in herself and others was a gift to our entire group. Because of this I hated to see her leave, yet, as I tell all the people with whom I work, therapy provides them with tools to make their life better and is not a life-time project.

Pat was in therapy for almost two years. Her problem was so unique and different that I asked her for special permission to share it with you. I think it shows in a very dramatic way what can be accomplished through therapy.

Ronnie graduated from therapy after a year. As you will see, his accomplishments were many.

ELLEN

ELLEN—Tonight I want to announce that next week will be my last week in therapy. So, I want to share things that I've gotten in touch with while in therapy and what I've accomplished. One thing I have learned is how important it is for me to be assertive. When I first came to therapy I used to go along with anything and everything people told me. If my husband or boss would criticize me I would just feel miserable. Instead of saying anything, I would get super migraine headaches. Because of my headache I would have to lay off work for several days and that would make things worse for me, as well as persecute my boss and husband . . . hmm . . . when I first came to therapy I was a mess!

MAY—Hey, I thought you were supposed to be telling us about the good things that you have accomplished, and not put yourself down.

ELLEN—[Laughter.] You're right. I was just thinking about it, though, and I really do feel good—you know, like the Virginia Slims commercial, "You've come a long way, baby."

Doris—You really have. You have worked hard.

MAY—That's true.

Doris—Tell us more about what you've accomplished.

ELLEN—Right. I like doing this. So what I first learned was that it was okay for me to check out what other people expected of me.

BRUCE—I don't want to sound mean, but when I hear you talking about how much you've changed I feel like you're putting me on. It sounds good, but . . .

MAY—I know how you feel, Bruce. I remember when I first came to group there was a woman who left who was saying how wonderful group was and how great she felt. I remember thinking two different kinds of thoughts. I felt she was too much, like she was putting me on (laughs). I also remember thinking that maybe she was a plant, Doris, you know, someone who was put in here to sell me on group. [Group laughter]—I also remember thinking, "Wow, if she can get that from group, I can too."

BRUCE—Yeah, that's what I feel.

Doris—Since Bruce is new in the group, Ellen, maybe it would help if you told us how the group helped you accomplish the things you're telling us.

ELLEN—Would that help, Bruce?

BRUCE—Yeah. I mean it sounds so . . .

MAY—Magical?

BRUCE—[Laughter] Right.

ELLEN—What I first learned about was that it was important to check out what other people wanted from me. The first day in group I was very nice and came on with all sorts of *nice* advice. Well, before the first group was over I was confronted three times for Rescuing. People didn't want me to be giving advice. Also, what I found out about me was that I didn't want all that syrupy advice either.

Doris—I remember.

ELLEN—I then started to check out, little by little, what my husband and boss expected of me. It was scary—believe me. But it was easier than having to live in a state of anxiety and fear wondering if I was being a good wife or a good secretary. Another thing I learned was that what I think and feel count. The group really helped me. I was astonished that when I made comments people in here listened and were very stroking and were mad when I didn't say anything. Also, when I would talk about things I was doing that I didn't want to do for people outside of group, the group was angry that I was discounting myself. What really got that message across, Alan, was that day in group when you asked me to tell you something I liked about you and I did. Then someone said that I didn't sound like I meant what I said. But what got me, Alan, was when you said I sounded phony. Finally, I admitted that I really hadn't wanted to stroke you. What really upset me, Alan, was your saying how much more hurt you were that I had given you a stroke when I didn't want to than if I had said, "No, I don't want to give you a stroke." I then realized that I would feel that same way. That was a turning point for me. I then started saying "no" outside of group. I found that I didn't have to bake a cake for church, or sell tickets, or head up every committee I was asked to serve on. It was great to find out that I could say "no" and I wouldn't be abandoned, especially by my husband. From there I have learned to express myself—to say what I like and don't like. If people discount me, I don't grin and bear it, I tell them about it. I remember when I confronted you, Doris, about starting the group late one night.

Doris—I remember it, too. [Laughter.]

GROUP—[Laughter.]

ELLEN—Well, that was a big step for me. You didn't fall apart or get mad. You said it was a good confrontation. Then one other time I confronted someone who did get mad at me, Doris, and you helped me see that I didn't have to back down. I was right and it was the other person's problem that he got angry. All of those experiences helped me see that I can stand up for myself. And it's been good. Not only for me, but also in my relationship with Jim, my husband. I admit we had some hard times at first because he wasn't used to my being assertive. He does see that I don't have migraine headaches now. We both recognize what the other wants. And that's because we tell each other what we want. We have stopped guessing what each wants from the other. Our relationship is so much more relaxed.

JERRY—Wow! So much assertion.

ELLEN—Right. It has made such a difference for me to tell people what I want instead of hoping they will simply know. I used to spend half my time feeling lousy because I didn't get what I wanted, but then I never asked. As a result of therapy I have changed a lot of things. I feel better—a lot better. And one of the things that I have realized is that I have a lot more control over my life than I ever thought possible.

JERRY—That's a nice illusion to have. [Laughter].

Doris—That's a kick, Jerry.

JERRY—No, I didn't mean it as a kick.

Doris—If you disagree with Ellen, say it in a straight way. The way you said that was a kick.

JERRY—Okay . . . yeah . . . let's see . . . I *doubt* that people have control over their own lives.

ELLEN—Well, I have more control than I thought I could have and that's really made a difference in my life. I'm not as anxious. I've learned I have lots of control over my feelings. If I feel sad about something, I don't have to feel sad for weeks on end. I feel sad for a day at the most. Then I figure out what's going on and do something for myself. Other people don't determine how I feel. *I* determine how I feel. I can turn on or off any feeling I want. I can start thinking about something scary and start feeling scared. Or I can get myself all sad or mad. I can make myself feel or not feel.

Doris—That's really said in a clear way, Ellen.

ALAN—Ellen, it's really been neat to see the way you've changed. When you first came to group, you usually looked sad and were very quiet. Now you're radiant. That makes me happy for you and also encouraged for myself.

CHUCK—I'm happy for you also, Ellen. For me, too; seeing you change shows me that I can change too.

Doris—I feel very warm towards you, Ellen. Also, I admire the way you have worked in this group. You listen to people . . . you give good feedback. You don't hold back. You take responsibility.

MARCY—You've changed so much.

GLORIA—I think it's just great. I remember that you never used to smile. You must have such good feelings for yourself, like you have climbed to the top of a mountain.

PHYLLIS—I'm really happy for you, Ellen. Also, it gives me courage to change myself.

BRUCE—I'm feeling sad that you're leaving group just when I'm coming in, but I'm really glad that you've done such good work. I'm optimistic for myself.

GROUP—Yeah!! Me too!

ELLEN—Thank you. I'll remember each of you and what you have given to me. Also, what I've given to myself.

HERB—So let's plan Ellen's graduation party.

Doris—Right on.

PAT

PAT—I'm ready to graduate from the group. How about that!

MIKE—Good. I'm up for a graduation party!

PEG—I agree.

Doris—Okay, Pat. If you are ready to leave the group, I'd like for you to go over your original goals and tell us what you've accomplished.

PAT—Okay. My goals when I first came into therapy were to work an eight hour day instead of sixteen hours a day and to get myself involved in at least two good relationships. I accomplished these goals some time ago. However, the big news is that I no longer have a dietary problem.

CAROL—What do you mean?

PAT—Well, as many of you know, I could never eat anything that contained any dairy product. So that eliminated a lot of stuff. Like no ice cream, butter, mayonnaise, sour cream, cake, even pretzels, because they are made with lactose. It was everything I liked. And what Doris told me was that when I started believing that *I* was an okay human being and really counted, and when I started allowing myself to trust people and ask for what I want, and get what I want, my allergy would probably disappear. Well . . . it did.

Six weeks ago I had two spoons of a sundae that Marsha, a friend of mine, was eating, and I didn't get sick. So the next day I had a glass of milk and there were no ill effects.

Doris—Last week Pat came into the office for an individual session eating a pint of tapioca.

GROUP—[Laughter.]

JIM—That's fantastic! How long have you had the allergy, Pat?

PAT—About seven years.

SUSAN—How did you know that Pat would get over the allergy when she got what she wanted, Doris?

Doris—Well, about a year ago, Pat told me that she had eaten some sour cream on her potatoes and it didn't affect her. I also knew that her allergy developed when she was in college. So, I decided that it was probably psychosomatic. Later, I put that together with the information that Pat had never allowed herself to be happy and get what she wanted. I also knew that when Pat was a child, ice cream was her favorite food. So, during one session I explained to Pat that I thought her allergy was psychosomatic and was a way for her to reinforce the idea that she would never get what she wanted. I also told Pat that when she started to allow herself to get what she wanted, the allergy would probably disappear. And, sure enough, Pat is now allowing herself to get what she wants and the allergy is gone.

PAT—I love it. I'm also doing well at my job. I'm working eight, sometimes nine hours a day, but no more sixteen hour days. And they still think I'm worth my salary.

Doris—Are you?

PAT—You bet!! I'm also meeting and socializing with lots more people and rarely feel depressed. My only problem now is that I'm starting to gain weight.

SUSAN—Listen, you can afford it. Man, you're ready to graduate!

GROUP—[Gives lots of strokes to Pat.]

MIKE—What about the party?

Doris—All right. Who will bring what?

MIKE—I'll bring cheese and sausage.

PEG—I'll bring bagels.

CAROL—I'll bring some deviled eggs.

Doris—Put me down for a bottle of wine.

LES—I could bring ice cream.

GROUP—[Laughter.]

Doris—Well, we'll meet for the first hour as usual, and there is no place to keep the ice cream, unless you can bring it with dry ice.

LES—Yeah. I'll bring some dry ice.

GROUP—Neat . . . great . . . oh, good!

PAT—I love it!

SUSAN—I'll make brownies.

Doris—Um, good.

JIM—Let's see. I haven't decided yet what I'll bring. Well, how about some fruit? I can get some apples from a farmer who lives near us. Okay. I'll bring apples.

BUDDY—And I'll bring some special Italian bread.

Doris—Wow! Then I'll have a dietary problem to work on.

GROUP—[Laughter.]

RONNIE

Doris—Ronnie, since today is your Graduation Day, I'd like you to give feedback about what you've gotten out of the group.

RONNIE—Fine. What I got out of the group is I've become undepressed, if there is such a word. I don't go into a "poor me, life is not worth living" position. I don't lay around like I used to. When I feel down, I figure out what I'm sad or mad about and then I do something. In other words, I get my "ass in gear."

GROUP—[Laughter.] That's neat!

RONNIE—I've also discovered that it's okay to get angry. I always used to think that it was very bad to get angry. I thought it was stupid to get angry, like it was a waste of time. When I first came into group, I was afraid of my anger and afraid of other people's anger. Now I'm able to be angry. You once told me, Doris, that depression was often anger turned inward. Well, I believe it, because when I get angry, I don't feel depressed. I'm also able to be more assertive. I thought assertiveness was bad. I thought to be completely passive was where it was at. I used to identify being passive and quiet with being very good and very righteous. I was very righteous all right!

GROUP—[Laughter.]

Doris—And very passive.

GROUP—[Laughter.]

RONNIE—I was also righteous in that I thought I had no problems. Then when I finally admitted my problems, I thought my problems were better than everyone else's and different. I had better problems! Imagine! A lot of people have problems around sex and I haven't had sexual problems, so I put myself up on a pedestal and said, "Well, since I don't have that problem, I'm better than others."

GROUP—[Laughter.]

RONNIE—I can make decisions now. Since I've been in the group, I've gone ahead with my divorce . . . I got a new apartment, bought a car, got my bills paid up . . . have started dating two neat gals . . . and have made a decision to go to graduate school in the fall. I think these are pretty big accomplishments.

Doris—I agree. It has been very rewarding to have watched you change.

LYNN—It also gives me hope that I will graduate.

BOB—How long have you been in the group?

RONNIE—Let's see, almost a year and a half. Even now, I don't want to leave. If Doris would let me continue in group with the condition that I didn't have to pay, I'd stay on.

Doris—[Laughter] No deal, Ronnie!

GROUP—[Laughter.]

III
EVERY MOLEHILL
IS A MOUNTAIN

Everything we do, no matter how small, affects the way we relate to each other. Every molehill has a potential for turning into a mountain. Let's suppose your guests, Sally and Bud, come forty-five minutes late for your well-planned dinner party. Seems trivial, but is it really?

The roast is well-done instead of pinkish as you and your husband like. By the time you serve your speciality, twice baked potatoes, they are glue-like in texture and resemble thrice baked potatoes.

Later in the evening, while discussing the Equal Rights Amendment, you find yourself being very vehement about what you are saying to Bud. You hear your voice heighten. In fact, it sounds as though you are engaged in battle. As you become aware of your voice, you also realize that your other guests have fallen silent and are watching you. Suddenly the molehill has turned into a mountain. The angry feelings you held back when the guests were late and the dinner was ruined have now surfaced while talking to Bud.

Another molehill which can and does become a mountain among people is the issue of smoking. I myself am very irritated by cigarette smoke and dislike when people insist on smoking in front of me. I do not want to breathe their smoke. Nor do I want my hair, draperies, sofa, kitchen, or office to smell like stale smoke. Too bad for me if I happen to be with a smoker. Most people do not check out how I feel about smoking, but automatically light up. They blow smoke here and there— mostly in my face. My eyes become red, my nose stuffy, and my house stinky. This happens because smokers believe that what they want is more important than what I want. In reality, smoking is not a need, it is a want. People can and do survive without cigarettes.

I must confess, however, that in a social situation, even if I am asked if I mind, I am hard put to say, "Yes, I do mind if you smoke." There is a great deal of social pressure not to say what I want and to discount my own feelings when a smoker expresses the desire to smoke. However, each time I discount myself I feel some mild irritation with that person. As this irritation—anger—continues to build, our relationship becomes more stressful. So the molehill of cigarette smoking has mushroomed into a mountain.

In this chapter I will show how seemingly insignificant issues such as being late, smoking in front of nonsmokers, or continuously interrupting others who are talking, often snowball into bigger issues if they are not dealt with.

If you watch television or read many mystery novels, you have probably encountered situations where someone is contemplating suicide. It is true that people do contemplate, and sometimes succeed in, killing themselves. Most people find an alternative and continue to live out their lives; however, the alternative may not deal with the problem(s) which motivated the suicidal desire.

When Frank first came into group he was very depressed, out of a job, and felt that things were "closing in on him." He talked about his worthlessness and his desire to do away with himself. He kept repeating to the group that his parents knew he would never make anything of himself, and they were right.

Martha, another group member, confronted Frank on his game of "Poor Me"[13] and told him that *he, not* his parents, was responsible for what he does with his life in the present and in the future. So he had better get his "ass in gear," find a job, and start making something of his life. At first Frank reacted defensively, but I told him to think about what Martha had said. He came back to the next group session and responded postively to Martha's confrontation.

The following week he announced that he had gotten a job, not a particularly good one, but one that he would stay with until he could find something better. For awhile Frank continued to work in group and seemed to have made a decision to give up the idea that he would never make it. Then one day he announced that he was fed up and was going to quit his job. The following transcript shows how Frank became aware of how he was setting up his life in a way to again justify doing away with himself. Frank's quitting his job, seemingly a molehill, was really a mountain in disguise.

A DECISION TO LIVE

FRANK—I think a need to work in the group today cause I have a, ah . . .

Doris—You *think* you need to work?

FRANK—No. I want to work. I have decided to quit my job. I think I need to talk about quitting because of where I'll be financially . . . um, and I'll probably be quitting my job this afternoon. I know I have good reasons for quitting. I don't know if I want to tell you my reasons for quitting so I can get people to tell me, "Yeah, quit"; or whether I want to deal with feeling scared because I won't have a job.

Doris—What you're doing right now is addressing all of our Parents in order that we tell you what you should do, Frank. What do you want to do?

FRANK—Okay. I want to deal with my feelings about quitting and how to handle things after I quit. I want to quit. I want to do what I want to do.

Doris—How will you feel after you quit?

FRANK—I'm going to feel really depressed. First scared, then depressed.

Doris—Why are you going to be scared?

FRANK—Cause I won't be able to take care of myself. I only have about three hundred in the bank and no relatives or girl friend to lean on for cash; so I'll be real scared.

Doris—And then what?

FRANK—And then, if that goes on long enough, having no job I mean, my Adult tells me it could go on for awhile with the unemployment situation like it is, then I'm going to get angry because no one is giving me a job. I'll get *really* angry.

Doris—Crazy society! Huh? Is that what you'll say?

FRANK—Yeah, they're not okay and then . . . uh . . . then I'll get depressed.

Doris—First you'll feel scared that you can't take care of yourself, then you'll get angry because you can't find another job and nobody's okay. Then you get depressed, turn your anger inward. Then what?

FRANK—Then what? I don't know. Then I'll just be depressed, I guess.

Doris—And when you feel depressed what happens?

FRANK—Let's see. When I feel that depressed, it's a good reason to die.

Doris—Suicide?

FRANK—Yeah.

SHIRLEY—You'd better not kill yourself Frank! You'd better not because it would really scare me. Also, I don't want you to kill yourself because I really like you.

Doris—Wait a minute, Shirley. That is a very caring thing to say to Frank, but he needs to work on this himself right now.

SHIRLEY—Okay. I see that.

Doris—So you're settin' it up, Frank, so that you can get the ultimate payoff in your life, which is to kill yourself.

FRANK—Well, that doesn't mean that my decision to quit my job is wrong. It just means I need to figure out how to handle what comes after quitting in a better way, so that it doesn't necessarily lead to suicide.

Doris—I think quitting your job without having another job to go to is a setup for you to ultimately feel angry enough to justify knocking yourself off. I don't want you to knock yourself off. So what do you need to do, Frank?

ED—Why do you want to quit?

Doris—Wait a minute. I want Frank to respond to what I said.

FRANK—Well . . . I . . . uh . . . I need to find another job before I quit. Yeah, I can agree with the fact that I shouldn't quit until I have another job. I did agree with that idea up until a couple of days ago. Now I just have so much anger and I'm afraid that with all the anger I'm feeling about the job, and about wanting to quit, if I don't quit until I find another job, I'm just really going to be pissed at you, Doris.

Doris—Okay. So when that happens you can deal with your anger at me with the double chair technique. [Frank will sit in one chair and talk to an empty chair representing

Doris.] Then I don't set myself up as a Victim and you can express your anger in a constructive way.

FRANK—Yeah . . . Okay . . . I want to make a contract. [A contract[14] is an agreement between the therapist and the fellow traveler to accomplish a clearly stated goal.]

Doris—So what's the contract?

FRANK—Okay. The contract is that I won't quit this job until I have another one. Okay, and next week I'll work on what pisses me off at work, or if there's time, I'll work on it today.

Doris—Okay. What about suicide?

FRANK—No suicide! I will restate my contract that I will not kill myself either directly or indirectly.[15]

LINDA—You have a fine Adult, Frank.

Doris—I feel really glad about the way you came through for yourself.

SHIRLEY—I feel relieved.

During that week and the weeks that followed, Frank continued to work on his feelings of self-worth. To his surprise, he found that he was considered an asset in the group and that his feedback to other group members was respected and valued. As he became more self-assured he found a better job. He stopped playing his "Poor Me" game and started concentrating on other issues that he needed to solve once he had made the decision to live.

Today Frank is leading a very productive life. He has a steady girl friend, a nice apartment and has been given two substantial raises in the past year. It's rare now when Frank thinks about giving up and as he says, "I know I can make it, and I will continue to make something of my life."

❖❖❖❖❖❖❖❖❖❖❖❖❖❖❖❖❖❖❖❖❖

From birth all of us receive directions as to how we should behave, what we should think, and how we should feel. The specific directions about how we should behave, think, and feel are referred to as parental messages.[16]

Throughout our life all of us follow various parental messages. Many of these messages are good and have helped us to survive and get what we want. However, other messages are destructive and often keep us from getting what we want. One of the reasons people come for therapy is to find out why their lives seem to be going so poorly and what they can do to make their life better. When people come to me for therapy one of the first things I do is work with them to help them find out what their parental messages are.

One of the group members in the next transcript is a girl named Sara. Using Sara as a model, I will go over what her parental messages were and how she was setting up her life to follow those messages.

Sara was told all her life by parents and teachers, either directly or indirectly, that she was stupid; so when Sara came into therapy she thought and acted as though she were stupid. When faced with a difficult situation which called for thinking, Sara considered herself *too stupid* to think and solve the problem. In TA we would say that Sara had followed her parental message, "Be Stupid." Other destructive parental messages that Sara had were: Little girls don't yell, fight, or get mad (Don't Be Angry); Come to us when you have a problem, Sara (Don't Think); Always have a smile on your face (Be Glad); You'll never amount to anything (Mess Up); and Money is the most important thing (Marry a Rich Man).

Next, Sara and I talked about whether she wanted to change these messages and, if so, what she would actually have to do to change them.

When Sara first came into group it took her an inordinate amount of time, seven weeks in fact, to learn the names of the other eight group members. She was exhibiting her "Be Stupid" message. Although at first not remembering people's names seemed like a molehill and not significant, this behavior was indicative of her "Be Stupid" message which was a real mountain in her life.

Therapists have various ways to help people find out their parental messages. In the next transcript one of the group members, Jan, who had been working on one of her parental messages, "Don't Have Fun," came to group with a party game she wanted to play in the group. Even though I had already worked with all the people in the group to identify their parental messages, it was interesting what I found out when my secretary gave me the typed transcript of the group session in which the group had played the party game. Almost everyone's parental messages could be identified by their comments. Although I did not confront what other people were saying at the time, nor was I aware of my own comments, I did analyze our conversations later. Following the transcript of the party game I have presented my analysis of what each of us said and how it revealed parental messages.

As you read the transcript, see if you can solve the puzzle before the answer is given.

SOLVE THE PUZZLE

JAN—I'll work. As you know, I have been working on becoming more free with myself and not being so stiff and having more fun. So last week I told some jokes and this week I have a game I want the group to play.

Doris—Neat.

GROUP—[Laughter.]

JAN—The thing is you have to guess a puzzle. Here's how it goes: I'm going on a trip to Canada and I'm going to take with me a pair of jeans and some nuts. You tell me two things that you're going to take on this trip, and I'll tell you if you can go or not. It all depends if you guess the right things. We'll go around the room until someone figures out what the answer to the puzzle is.

Doris—Okay. You've already given us two of the pieces, a pair
   of jeans and some nuts.

JAN—Right.

DAN—I'll take along some tennis shoes and a rope.

JAN—No.

Doris—Three sleeping bags and four cans of beans.

JAN—No.

GROUP—[Laughter.]

SARA—Gloves and ski equipment.

JAN—No.

GROUP—[Laughter.]

MICK—Shoes and two pizzas.

JAN—No.

GROUP—[More laughter.]

Doris—Now what happens?

JAN—Now I'll add some more things.

MICK—Will this tell us more about the puzzle?

JAN—Yes.

MICK—Good, another clue.

SARA—This will give us another clue about the puzzle, but this time with different words.

JAN—Yes. This time I'm gonna take along some jelly and a nutcracker.

LYNN—Okay. Peanut butter and Traveler's Checks.

JAN—No, you can't go along.

SARA—You don't seem to spend much money on your trip.

GROUP—[Laughter.]

DAN—I'll take some stew and a pair of socks.

JAN—No.

Doris—I thought you had it. Something to eat and something to wear.

GROUP—[Laughter.]

Doris—Okay, not a nutcracker, jelly and jeans. Huh . . . Oh, brother . . . a bottle of wine and a ring.

JAN—No.

LYNN—Jan, if one of the items is right, would you say, "yes" to that?

JAN—No, both items have to be right.

LYNN—But you don't indicate if one is right. You say, "no" even though one may be correct.

JAN—Yes.

LYNN—We may have each said one thing that fit, but we immediately wiped it out by saying a wrong thing.

JAN—Yes.

SARA—Okay, wine and bread?

JAN—No.

MICK—Jars and a nickel?

JAN—No.

GROUP—[Laughter.]

Doris—I know what you thought the puzzle was, "J" and "N." That was very clever, Mick.

JAN—This time I'm gonna bring a jawbreaker and a . . . [long pause].

Doris—How about a needle, Jan?

JAN—Yes, a needle.

Doris—Are you *sure* Mick hasn't figured out the puzzle, Jan?

JAN—No.

GROUP—[Laughter.]

MICK—No, you're not sure?

JAN—No, I *am* sure. You didn't guess the puzzle, Mick.

LYNN—I'm gonna bring boots and a walking stick.

JAN—Um . . . no.

MICK—Coconut and some thread.

JAN—No.

GROUP—[Laughter.]

Doris—Noodles and a jar to keep them in.

JAN—No.

GROUP—[Laughter.]

MICK—That'll teach you, switching around the letters "J" and "N."

GROUP—[Laughter.]

SARA—Compass and a flag.

JAN—No.

MICK—A sandwich and a sweater.

JAN—No . . . let's see . . . I'm gonna take along . . .

Doris—Would it help us if we wrote what you took along on the board?

JAN—It might.

Doris—First thing you mentioned was jeans and nuts.

JAN—Then I said jawbreaker and a needle.

MICK—Oh for heaven's sake!! This is impossible!

JAN—No it's not. This time I'm gonna bring along January month and a needle again. January month and a needle.

Doris—We can't be defeated by this game. One more time around.

LYNN—I wish I were sitting where you are, Jan.

MICK—I'm going to take a jump rope.

GROUP—[Laughter.]

MICK—A jump rope and a needle.

JAN—No.

MICK—No?

GROUP—[Laughter.]

JAN—It's not "J" and "N." That's not the answer.

Doris—Hmm . . . syllables don't seem to play a part, nor singular and plural.

LYNN—She said "nuts" first and "nutcracker" later. That was something you could eat and then a utensil to get it open.

Doris—I think you're right. Okay, January month and a needle. Okay, what can I do with January month? I'm going to take a coat which I would need in January and some thread.

JAN—No.

GROUP—[Laughter.]

MICK—I have a feeling when this is all over that I'm going to be ready to kill all of you. This has got to be something utterly ridiculous.

GROUP—[Laughter.]

Doris—Fun and games, remember? That's Jan's contract.

JAN—Are any of you ready to give up?

GROUP—No!. [Laughter.]

SARA—I just can't see anything that fits.

MICK—How about a jacket and a needle?

JAN—No.

MICK—Gloves and books.

JAN—No.

MICK—Okay. I give up.

Doris—Tell us what it is.

JAN—I'll give you two things that you would bring along, Doris.

Doris—Okay . . . Oh . . . What *I* would bring along. So it has something to do with each of us as individuals.

JAN—Yes. You would bring along a dime and a scarf. Mick, you would bring along some money and a kazoo. It's the first and last letter in your first name.

Doris—Oh, so Sara you might bring along a saw and an acorn. If you had said saw and an acorn and she would have said "right," and I would have thought you both had bats in belfrey.

GROUP—[Laughter.]

MICK—That's clever, Jan.

Doris—That's a neat game. I really like it; and you did a good job. You sure turned me on.

LYNN—I enjoyed it also.

DAN—Fun, Jan.

Did you guess the answer before Jan told us? Before you go on, one more question: Which of the players do you see yourself as being like? Now I will give my analysis of what transpired in the group and how our comments and behavior gave clues to our parental messages.

Let's first check the comments Mick makes. First he guesses shoes and a pizza. Then he asks Jan about more clues. Next he puts together the pattern "J" and "N" and guesses jars and a nickel. Even though Jan tells him his guess is incorrect, he checks it out again with her. His next guess is a coconut and thread. Then he laughs at *my* not catching onto the game. Mick then gives it one more try with a sandwich and a sweater. After Jan's confirmation that he hasn't figured out the game yet he decides it's impossible, but then he is back again with one more try . . . a jump rope and a needle. He continues to persist with his "J" and "N" even though he was told earlier that that was not the answer. He now informs us that when the game is over he will be ready to kill all of us; but once more the old college try, and there is another guess with the letters "J" and "N"— jacket and a needle. His final try is gloves and books. In the end he strokes Jan's cleverness.

Mick is a guy who never gives up. He gets mad at defeat, but comes right back again. The thing that often stands in his way in therapy is his refusal to hear when he is wrong. Often he continues to argue about being right long after it is obvious that he is wrong, as he did with his persistence in using the letters "J" and "N." In summary, Mick's messages that were revealed in this game are: Work Hard, Don't Give Up, Don't Be Wrong, Look for Other's Faults, and Be Perfect.

Sara, who was described at the beginning of the chapter, as usual takes a more passive role than other group members. Her first guess is gloves and ski equipment. Her next intervention is a question which has just been answered. Sara's comments reinforce to herself and the group that she is stupid. She then comments on the fact that Jan doesn't spend much money on her trips, an obvious put-down which is intended to make Sara okay and Jan not okay. Sara then takes a guess—wine and bread. Next a compass and a flag. Finally, she gives up, smiles, and stops playing. As you can see, Sara has acted out a number of her destructive parent messages that were presented earlier; such as, Be Stupid, Don't Think, Mess Up, Don't Be Angry, Money is the Most Important Thing.

What Dan does during the game is equally revealing. He

starts out by taking one guess and doesn't come back into the game until it has ended. His last comment is a stroke to Jan. Two of his parent messages are that he is to "Be Perfect" and "Be a Nice Guy." Because Dan doesn't take a chance, he doesn't have to be wrong. What better way to continue to operate under the illusion of "being perfect," and remain a nice guy as well, by stroking Jan at the end of the game.

Lynn spends the majority of her time figuring out the rules instead of playing the game. She takes two guesses, but makes four comments about the game. In everyday life she joins committees, works for good causes, and runs away from facing her marriage and children. Some of her parent messages are: Don't Be Close, Work Hard, Don't Show Your Feelings, and Be an Achiever.

My own comments during the game are also revealing. I immediately try to figure things out as I ask Jan if she has already given us two pieces of the puzzle with her first statement. Then I am off and running. I take five guesses and ask six questions to clarify what we are looking for. I also give six strokes in the group. In addition, I say, "We can't be defeated by this game; one more time around." As can be seen, my parent messages are: Work Hard, Don't Give Up, You're Responsible to Get the Job Done, Be Glad, and Keep Things Moving. In my life, I continually try to solve problems and have a difficult time giving up—an asset and a liability.

❖❖❖❖❖❖❖❖❖❖❖❖❖❖❖❖❖❖❖❖❖❖❖❖❖

On to the next molehill . . . in this transcript the molehill is a simple question, the mountain is all the information that follows. Marty asks Judy, "Why do you want to divorce your husband?" The question never gets answered, but what it does is to help Marty figure out why he is always asking questions. It also serves as a springboard to help Alan figure out why he always expects himself and others to answer *all* questions asked.

IT WAS JUST A SIMPLE QUESTION

MARTY—Why do you want to divorce your husband, Judy?

JUDY—I don't think I can answer that question in twenty-five words or less [stated angrily].

MARTY—I just asked the question, that's all.

Doris—Marty, how did you feel when Judy said to you, "I don't think I can answer that in twenty-five words or less."

MARTY—Well, I didn't feel like she was "out to get me?"

Doris—Then how come you used the words "out to get me"?

MARTY—Well, maybe I was mad because she didn't answer my question. Maybe a little sad. No, not sad. Let's stick with the mad. I felt mad.

Doris—Okay Judy, the way you answered Marty was a kick.[17]

JUDY—I was angry. I don't understand why I should have to explain my divorce to him or anyone else.

MARTY—I think maybe you're right that you don't have to explain things to me. I'm really sorry that I asked. It was just that I wanted to know.

Doris—Hold on. You're in your overadapative compliant Child, Marty. Get into your Adult. What you said was, "You don't have to explain it to me, but I want to know." I think it's okay for you to ask another group member any question you want. If they choose not to answer, it's okay for them to say that. I might ask how come they're choosing not to answer, but I think it's all right for you to ask. How could you have responded to Marty without kicking, Judy?

JUDY—I could have said, "I don't want to answer that question, Marty." And I apologize for the kick.

MARTY—Okay. I would like to check something out regarding myself. At times I do ask questions that rub people the wrong way and they turn off and get mad at me; but I really want to know the answers [said strongly]. I find I keep wanting more information.

Doris—If Judy had answered your question, Marty , what other things would you want to know?

MARTY—I would want to know, what were the things about her husband that got her pissed off? Did she reach a point in her relationship where she just decided, "I just don't want to be married to him"?

Doris—Those are good questions, Marty. Let me check something out about your past. How many kids are in your family?

MARTY—Listen, I'm the last one of nine.

Doris—Will you give me the approximate ages of your brothers and sisters when you were born?

MARTY—Let's see. My oldest brother was twenty-four. Then I had another brother twenty, and a brother nineteen, and a sister eighteen, and a brother seventeen. And then my folks must have decided to take a rest [laughter]. Then there were twins, age nine, and then Kathy, age six, and then me.

Doris—How old were your parents when you came along?

MARTY—My Mom was forty-four and my Dad was forty-seven.

Doris—Did they want another child?

MARTY—I really don't know.

Doris—Yeah Marty, you know. Kids know if they are wanted or not.

MARTY—I think they did.

Doris—You *think* they did?

MARTY—Yeah. I think they did, with doubts.

Doris—Okay. Would you say, "I hope they did, Doris."

MARTY—I hope they did [uncomfortable laughter].

Doris—Okay, here's my theory. Forty-four year old Mom and forty-seven year old Dad with all the kids in school and "whamo," all of a sudden a new baby arrives and they have to start all over. Up in the middle of the night, changing diapers again, and wiping up messes. You have children, Marty, so you know about those hassles. I'm thinking that your Mom and Dad might have been angry about having another baby. So, if your Mom is hassled by her teenagers, and a one month old baby, by the time that one month old gets to be two, three, or four years old and is into asking all kinds of curious questions—"How come, Mom?"—and keeps these questions up, I don't know if those questions would get a response. My fantasy is that you had a lot of questions when you were a little kid, as all little kids do, and that those questions weren't answered. And you also got some angry vibes whenever you asked those questions.

MARTY—That sounds right. I've always been known as someone who's always asking questions and getting people angry with me.

Doris—So you ask people too many questions, which rubs them the wrong way, and then you don't get your questions answered. Thus, you are recreating the same situation that happened in childhood.

MARTY—That certainly sounds like it fits. I'll just shoot this one thing off. When I was about nine or ten I found out about sex. And I used to ask my Mom all kinds of questions about sex, knowing that she would always tell me these fairy tales. She'd tell me nice things like "you were a miracle" and "you lived under my heart for nine months"—bull like that. I used to keep pressing her, and in the end she would get mad.

ALAN—If you were old enough to know you were getting the wrong answers, how come you kept asking the questions? I think that getting wrong answers is just as bad as getting no answers.

MARTY—Umm . . . Yeah, I guess.

Doris—Well, getting wrong answers is *not* the same as getting no answers. Marty learned how to get a lot of strokes from asking questions. First, Marty heard lots of good strokes from his Mom like, "You lived under my heart for nine months." Then, after Marty harassed her enough, Mom would become angry and give him negative strokes.

MARTY—Hmm . . . That's right. My asking questions was a way, and still is a way, to get strokes. It's not the answers that are important, it's the strokes.

DELORES—You really put that together well, Marty. What are you going to do with the information?

MARTY—I'm not sure. What I do know is that if I want to give up asking people so many questions, I'll have to figure out a better way to get people to give me strokes.

Doris—Right on. I do want to say that you have asked some good questions in here, so it's important that you use your Adult to decide when it's appropriate to ask a question.

MARTY—Yes, I can see that.

Doris—Also, suppose you make a list of ways that you can get strokes for yourself which will replace the strokes that you get from asking too many questions.

MARTY—All right. I'll do that and report to the group next week.

JUDY—Good work, Marty.

Doris—You're sitting there grinning, Alan. What is going on with you?

ALAN—Yeah, well, I got a real revelation out of Marty's story. I was the oldest of only two children, and I got *every* question answered by my parents or someone. So, when I got out into the big, wide, wonderful world, when I didn't get a question answered I really felt rejected because I had had all of my questions answered before.

DELORES—But you also act as though you *have to have* all of the answers.

ALAN—Yes, I realize now that I do feel angry when I ask a question and don't get an answer.

Doris—You feel angry if people don't answer questions. Umm

. . . the thing I want to pick upon is what Delores said about *you must have all the answers.*

ALAN—I don't understand. I must have all the answers? *You* think I should have, or *I think* I should have?

DELORES—When you first came into this group, you were very condescending and liked to put people down. You acted as though you were okay and nobody else was okay; and you used to do it by having all the answers.

ALAN—It goes further than that, too, in the sense that if I didn't get an answer I would be angry with that person and I would say, "that dumb head."

Doris—You have an expectation that people will come through for you with answers, but in addition you put that expectation on yourself and you say, "I gotta have all the answers."

ALAN—People expect me to have the answers and, damn it, I guess I expect other people and myself to have all the answers.

Doris—Alan, nobody needs to have all the answers, you don't have all the answers, and you don't need to have all the answers. It's your Parent inside your head that expects you to have all the answers, and it's your Child who expects everyone else to have all the answers.

ALAN—Yes, I'm finding that out.

Doris—I think you are. I have seen you do a lot of changing in this group.

ALAN—That's true. It's easier for me to say, "I don't know" and it doesn't upset me. I could never say, "I don't know" before I came to this group.

DELORES—I think that's neat.

ALAN—Yeah. I agree.

DELORES—I've seen you change in here also.

ALAN—People have asked me some of the damndest questions!

GROUP—[Laughter.]

Doris—And you don't need to have all the answers anymore.

ALAN—Right.

Doris—Now, what about all the "damndest questions" *you* have asked?

ALAN—I don't have to expect people to have all the answers either and then use this as a way to put them down when they don't. That's good to hear. You're right. I feel relieved. I'd like the group to call me on it if they see me into either one of those things.

GROUP—We will.

WHO DUN-IT?

Sam was a lawyer. He was forty-six, married, the father of three sons and one daughter. Two of his sons were attending well-known universities. His third son was a senior in high school, his daughter a sophomore. He had had his own firm up until two years before he came to see me in therapy. When his partner became ill, he decided to "call it quits" and join someone else's law firm and "not have so many responsibilities."

I still remember the first day he came into my office. Despite his thinning hair and his mid-forty paunch, he looked like a little boy about four years of age. He certainly would have seemed more in character to me if he had been carrying a teddy bear instead of a briefcase.

He came into my office, sat down in one of the gray chairs, squirmed around a little, smiled tensely, and cleared his throat. He then said he was coming to me because he had been thinking about committing suicide. He stated that he was unhappily married, dissatisfied with his job, and just couldn't get interested in anything. His main reason for continuing to live was that he felt his children cared about him and needed him, but sometimes he had doubts about that. In this first session, Sam made a verbal contract not to kill himself either directly or indirectly.

During the next two sessions Sam talked about his wife. He described Rosalie as physically attractive and bright. His main complaint was that they rarely talked and had had no sexual contact for the past two months. His wife had refused to come in to see me because she didn't trust doctors or "shrinks." After the third session Sam agreed to go into a therapy group. About the same time that Sam entered the group, my family and I moved into a new neighborhood.

It wasn't long until our boys were established in their new school and the phone started ringing with a voice at the other end shouting in excitment, "Can you come over and play?" Sometimes the phone would ring and there wasn't any voice, just a giggle. Other times the phone would ring and there would be no response to my "hello" except heavy breathing. I recall giving our children the message to tell their friends to stop calling and giggling or hanging up when I answered the phone. Both boys said they would, but my phone continued to ring with no one answering; there would be only the sound of breathing at the other end.

One evening, after returning from a dinner party, the phone rang at 11:50 P.M. Immediately I thought of my parents. Had there been an accident? Heaven knows what. With great apprehension I picked up the telephone only to hear heavy breathing at the other end. All of a sudden I knew. Those phone calls for the last several months! It wasn't the boys' friends at all. It was someone else. I started thinking and putting things together. It became clear that someone was harassing our family. But who?

Several days went by. No calls. Life continued as usual. Then, 5:05 A.M. on a Saturday morning the phone rang. Half awake, I reached for the phone and said, "Hello." I was greeted by a very angry woman on the other end of the phone. I listened intently to her voice, her words, and her pronunciation. She said angrily, "You bitch! Just who do you think you are? What are you trying to do, take him away from me?" She then made a loud growling noise and slammed the phone down. After she hung up and I thought about it, I decided it had to be the wife or girl friend of some man I was seeing in therapy. I bounded out of bed, grabbed my appointment book, and started flipping through the pages. Who was the angry caller? After some thought, I decided not to have my phone number changed, as this move would probably infuriate my already angry caller, and I didn't want her to escalate further. If she could harass me on the phone, she was less likely to try something else. After contacting the phone company, a tracer was placed on the phone. Of course, as luck would have it, the phone calls stopped. It was around a holiday, so perhaps she, too, had decided to take a vacation. The holiday weekend was finally over. Monday morning at 9:05 A.M. the phone rang. Hurrah! I was relieved. The phone company traced the call and quickly got back to me. I knew now who the mystery woman was— Sam's wife, Rosalie. I confronted Sam and said he needed to bring his wife in for a meeting soon with me and Carla, the co-therapist with me in Sam's group. If he failed to bring her in, I would press charges.

The reasons that she had been harassing me became evident in the first meeting. Her husband had been making all sorts of suggestions about the relationship he had with me, and Rosalie was furious with me. She thought I was taking her husband away. Also, since Sam had been coming to the group, his be-havior toward Rosalie had worsened, and consequently Rosalie saw it as my fault. She was not even aware that the group had a cotherapist because Sam had not bothered to mention this fact.

The following four transcripts of Sam working in therapy may seem like no big deal. So who cares if somebody uses cop-out words? . . . doesn't take responsibility? . . . doesn't answer questions? All molehills . . . but, oh brother . . . the mountains that these molehills did become.

ACT ONE

Carla—Did the answering service tell you that Lee wouldn't be here, Doris?

Doris—Yes, I got the message; but they didn't say why she wasn't coming to group. Do you know the reason she isn't here, Carla?

SAM—I'd like to work now, Doris.

Doris—Okay, Sam. But I'd like you to wait until after Carla answers my question.

Carla—Lee called and told me that she won't be here tonight because her husband, who has been out of town on business for the last three weeks, is coming home for several days; and she wants to spend as much time with him as possible, as he is to leave for South America for six weeks.

SAM—Carla, what's the chance of me working now?

Carla—Well, there's a good chance if you ask the right person that question. You asked Doris the first time, so you need to ask her again.

SAM—Okay, Doris, I'd like to work now.

Doris—I would like to talk about what happened between you and me just a few minutes ago, Sam. I confronted you and asked you to wait until Carla was finished talking. Then what happened was that when Carla finished talking you asked her if you could work. So you were setting up the game, "Let You and Him Fight";[18] and in this case, "Let Me and Carla Fight." First you addressed me, and then Carla. It looked as though you were invested in splitting us.

SAM—Huh? Who me . . . splitting you?

Carla—Yes. It's rare that someone addresses one of us specifically to work on a problem in therapy, and you did just that. I agree with Doris' analysis.

SAM—Well . . . I do remember that someone asked me to wait until they finished talking. Did you ask me to wait? I guess you did ask me to wait, Doris, until Carla was finished talking.

Doris—You are not responding to what I said, Sam. What did I say to you?

SAM—Well, you said Carla should finish talking before I should start to work.

Carla—That is not what Doris said.

SAM—Well, I don't know for sure. Did you say that I was trying to get the two of you to fight because I asked Doris about working, making her the important therapist, and then I asked Carla about working, making her the important therapist?

Doris—Did I say that?

SAM—Well, I'm really not sure. I guess, probably.

Doris—Did I?

SAM—Uh, yes . . . I think so.

Doris—And do you agree with the interpretation that I made and that you just repeated?

SAM—I don't recall feeling that I wanted the two of you to fight.

Doris—You didn't respond to my question, Sam.

SAM—Well, yes. I think the interpretation is correct . . . at least it sounds right.

Doris—Okay. How did you feel when I asked you to wait?

SAM—You mean, was I angry?

Doris—I don't know. What feeling did you have when you were asked to wait?

SAM—Um . . . [long pause].

Doris—Okay, we're all waiting so right now you are doing an angry thing by making us wait.

SAM—That's angry? I'm acting angry?

Doris—Yes. We're all sitting here waiting for you to get this issue resolved. You keep fooling around and fooling around. In the end the whole group will start feeling angry with you. So, if you would allow yourself to feel the anger and deal with it in a straight way when you feel it, you wouldn't, and we wouldn't, have to go through all this other stuff. What happened was that you were told to wait, so my guess is that you were angry with me, which would have been okay for you to feel. But you discounted your anger and you tried to get me back by getting Carla and me to fight. An now you're getting back at the group with your anger because we're all waiting for you to figure out what happened.

So that's very angry stuff, Sam.

SAM—That's angry stuff?

Doris—Okay. Game's over. When you are ready to tell the group what you did and take responsibility, we will work with you.

SAM—All right.

Later on in the group Sam came back in and said that he *had* been angry with me for making him wait and that it was difficult for him to say when he was angry. I then told Sam that people knew when he was angry by his behavior, and it would be appropriate for him to work on expressing his anger straight.

ACT TWO

MINI—Is there any reason why you've been so quiet in group tonight, Sam?

SAM—Me?

MINI—Yes.

SAM—I don't think I have been quiet. Well . . . uh . . . maybe tonight I have been quiet. Am I quiet? I don't know.

MINI—You avoid almost everything people say to you.

SAM—I'm avoiding something? Well, uh . . . I know I avoid showing anger. At least I think I do.

MINI—You don't avoid showing your anger, Sam. You show your anger all the time by doing angry things in this group. When you're confronted in here you *never take responsibility for yourself.* You don't make a statement, or if you do it's qualified. Everything is a question. You either repeat back what the person says or you ask it in a question form. So what happens is that the other person gets into taking responsibility for you, and if this goes on long enough we start feeling angry; so we take on your anger.

Carla—Do you understand that feedback?

SAM—I think I do, but I think I have had glimpses of my behavior before this.

Doris—We are into it again. You qualified your statement and then you kicked Mini by saying you already had glimpses about your behavior. So again people will be angry with you and take on your anger.

SAM—The group is helping me gain insight and I feel like that's progress.

Carla—Well, it's progress to know what's going on, but progress is not enough unless you do something with the information. So I would like you to think this week about the feedback you got in here tonight and then make a decision about what you're going to do with the information and how you will change your behavior.

SAM—Okay.

ACT THREE

The group session one week prior to finding out that it is Sam's wife who is making the harassing phone calls.

SAM—I'd like to work. I've thought a lot about what you said last week, Doris, and I do think that I act like a little boy with my wife and with other people. I sort of stand back and wait for other people to tell me what to do and I really don't like that about myself.

Doris—Well, you are smiling, Sam. That smile is a gallows smile.[19]

SAM—What do you mean . . . a gallows smile?

Doris—A gallows smile is your Child ego state smiling at some destructive or crazy thing you are doing in your life. The smile is called gallows because you are heading for some misfortune, perhaps the gallows, and you are smiling about it all the way. I think it's destructive that you set people up to tell you what to do and you also agree that you don't like that part about yourself, and yet you sit there smiling as you are telling us how you stand back and let other people tell you what to do.

SAM—I see. Okay . . . Well, I am starting to be assertive and I don't always act like a little boy.

Doris—What specific things are you doing, Sam? When are you taking a stand and not waiting for someone else to tell you what to do?

SAM—Well, I'm thinking about it a lot.

LEE—What are the things that you're *doing* to be assertive?

SAM—Well, I'm not doing as much as I could. I have worked out a beautiful exercise which helps me with my anger. I'll tell you about my exercise. I take two ten pound dumbbells in each hand and first lift them over my head and then I bring them down hard like this. [Sam demonstrates exercise.] First I started doing that fifty times and that was too much, so I didn't keep it up.

VERN—Why are you doing that exercise?

SAM—To get rid of some of the anger I feel at people, especially my wife.

VERN—And if you get rid of that anger, what's going to happen?

SAM—I'll get more energy to deal with things.

LEE—We started out with *what* are you *doing* to be assertive? Do you remember the question?

SAM—Yes.

LEE—What are some of the things you're doing in order to stop being a little boy and grow up? I'm still unclear as to what you're actually doing.

SAM—I'm searching out the games that I play and my wife plays.

Doris—What does that mean, "I'm searching out the games?" How is that helping you not be a little boy?

SAM—Well, I think games are not played with your Adult, are they?

Doris—Listen, Sam, you already know the answer. So tell us one thing that you have done this week to grow up.

SAM—Well, this evening when I was getting ready for group, Rosalie, my wife, said kind of nasty like, "*So* you're going out tonight." Her tone of voice was provocative, like she wanted to fight and I just didn't fall for it. I didn't get into a hassle with her.

Doris—What *did* you do?

SAM—Well, I didn't say anything.

Doris—Okay. You smiled in here when you told us about your wife's remark. So my guess is that you smiled when she said, "*So* you're going out tonight."

SAM—I smiled in here?

Doris—You had a smile on your face when you told us about her provocative comment to you. So I think that although you're not verbally fighting, giving her a smile was a way to egg her on. So what message were you giving your wife with your smile, Sam? Or, what message were you giving the group when you smiled as you were telling the story?

SAM—I'm not sure but the message could be, "I'm pulling one over on you." Is that what my smile would mean?

Carla—Is that what it means?

SAM—I don't know.

Doris—You know.

SAM—I think it means, yes, I guess that's what it means. I'm pulling one over on you, Rosalie.

Doris—Listen, Rosalie knows good and well where you go on Monday nights. So, if you had said, "Yes, I'm going to the group, and I know you don't approve" that would have been a straight transaction and no game. But, when you smile that's like saying, "I've got a secret," and the game is on. By smiling, Rosalie's Child has lots of encouragement from you, Sam, to have all sorts of fantasies about what goes on in your therapy group.

SAM—Yeah . . . I think I see what you mean.

Carla—What *are* you pulling over on Rosalie, Sam?

SAM—I don't know.

Doris—I want you to think about it.

ACT FOUR

The following week. Sam is confronted about his wife's telephone calls.

Doris—The reason that we asked you to stay after group tonight and have an individual session with us, Sam is that since sometime in November, or early December, I started getting harassing phone calls. In the last two months the calls got worse, so I . . .

SAM—From my wife?!? The phone calls are from my wife?

Doris—Yes.

SAM—Oh, for goodness sake.

Doris—It sounds to me like you must have known that she was calling me, since you came to that conclusion before I finished what I was saying.

SAM—Well, no. But I know that she isn't happy about my coming to therapy; but I never thought she would do something like that.

Doris—We know that the calls came from your house, because I had a tracer put on my phone. We can't say for sure it's your wife, but it is a female. So it's your wife or daughter, unless there is a housekeeper or aunt or another woman living with you.

SAM—No. And, it couldn't be my daughter. I can't imagine it being my daughter. I can imagine it being my wife because she's like crazy with jealousy and fear about the fact that I might divorce her.

Doris—Well, one of the things that Carla and I discussed when we learned it was your wife was that you might be feeding into her jealousy and fear in some way. So are you aware of anything that you're doing that would feed into her jealousy which in turn causes Rosalie to be angry with me?

SAM—Well, like you said, Doris, I don't say, "Yes, I'm going to group," but I smile; so then Rosalie can go ahead and let her fantasies run wild; but the reason I don't talk to her about group is because she gets so upset if I bring it up.

Doris—Okay. I'm still struck by how fast you jumped to the conclusion that it was your wife who was calling me. Have there ever been any incidents like this before, Sam?

SAM—No. I don't think so. I don't know of any time that Rosalie has used the telephone to harass someone.

Doris—What about letters? Has she ever written letters to anyone or said anything to anyone that you thought might be a form of harassment?

SAM—I have suspected it, but I don't know for sure.

Carla—You didn't act surprised at all when Doris told you that your wife was making harassing calls.

SAM—I may not have acted like it, but I'm surprised that she would go this far. I'm distrubed by it.

Carla—This is really sick behavior, Sam. And she's escalating her anger. She's been saying very bizarre things. Very crazy stuff to Doris on the phone. And now what we need to talk about is, what's the best way to deal with it so she doesn't escalate her anger any more.

Doris—Also, she needs to get help, and I think that's something you need to make very clear to her.

Carla—I think that both you and she should come to see Doris and me together. That way we can talk about her fantasies and also see how you are playing into the problem.

SAM—I don't know if she will come.

Doris—Well, I think you should demand it. She's going to get herself into a lot of legal trouble. The telephone company already has the information, my lawyer has the information, and he will prosecute if the calls continue. If that happens, she will lose her job. You know that. So, one way to avoid all that happening is for you to get her in here to see us so that she can see that nothing is going on between us, see that there is no hanky-panky, and that she doesn't have to be jealous or angry.

SAM—I'm sure she wouldn't come if I just plain asked her to come.

Doris—I agree with that, so what do you need to do?

SAM—Demand it. Demand that she come.

Carla—That's right. So you need to give her an ultimatum.

SAM—Couldn't it possibly be anybody else? It has to come from my house?

Doris—It's been traced, Sam . . . and you're starting to play games again.

SAM—Yeah, okay. It is Rosalie.

Doris—How are you going to handle this information when you get home? What are you going to do?

SAM—The calls are mostly to your home?

Doris—Yes and you are again avoiding the issue of what you are going to do when you get home.

SAM—I can hardly imagine all this. Well, I'll confront her with the information.

Doris—How are you going to do that? I'd like to hear how you're going to do it.

SAM—I'll ask her if she's been calling Doris.

Carla—That's the first move in the game of NIGYSOB. Do you understand that, Sam? You say, "Are you calling Doris" and she says, "No" and then you're going to say, "Well, I know you are calling her." So you've got her, you get to kick her. You need to go home and be in your Parent and your Adult and say, "I've got information that you've been calling Doris." You are also to tell her how you know. If she says, "That's not true" and starts escalating, you need to say, "Sit down, I want to tell you how I know." You've got to be tough, Sam, or you're going to get into a big game. She needs you to be in your Parent and Adult. You need to protect yourself and her and be in your Parent and Adult.

SAM—Yeah, I see.

Doris—Think about her like a two-year-old kid who needs to listen to what you have to say. You're doing it for her protection. That's why when you talk to a two-year-old, you don't reason with them, you tell them, "Don't cross the street." That's what she needs at this point. She must also be scared about what she's doing. She knows somewhere that her behavior is crazy. Most people want to be stopped from acting crazy.

SAM—Yeah. I can see that.

Doris—So you need to do that, Sam. You've got to be very powerful and give her an ultimatum.

SAM—I'll tell her she must stop her childish behavior.

Doris—No, don't blame or put her down.

SAM—What?

Doris—Don't blame it on her childish behavior.

SAM—Okay. "You must stop calling Doris, Rosalie, because it's harmful in many ways."

Carla—Bullshit! You sound about as powerful as a petunia. It's important for yourself and for her, Sam, that you don't sabotage talking with Rosalie. Right now you need to be strong for both of you. And you aren't going to do it with that kind of voice.

SAM—Okay. I will be strong.

Doris—So I want to hear how you're going to do it.

SAM—Rosalie, I have information that you are telephoning Doris. You know you can't do that. You must stop that. We will go to Doris and talk to her jointly if you want.

Doris—The last part is a con, Sam. "If you want to talk to Doris" is setting her up to say, "I don't want to." You *tell* her, "We are going to talk to Doris and get this thing straightened out" and you either go with me or . . . what?

SAM—You either go in with me or there will probably be some serious consequences.

Doris—Probably! I'm angry with you, Sam. Stop playing games now, Sam, this is real. This lady is to the point where she's not fooling around anymore, so you stop fooling around, too. Stop giving her ammunition to escalate. If she won't come in with you, what is your ultimatum?

SAM—It doesn't seem humane to threaten to divorce a sick person.

Carla—Is that your ultimatum? You will divorce her if she won't come?

SAM—Yes.

Carla—It is humane if you threaten that person to get help or you'll *divorce them. That's humane*, that's very humane, Sam, to use your power to get Rosalie to come through for herself.

Doris—Okay. Now I'm giving an ultimaum. You either deal with this appropriately and get Rosalie in here for a session with Carla, me, and you, or you're out of therapy with us. Permanently! I won't take the risk of working with you when you seem to care more about playing games than getting this issue solved. I won't care more than you care about solving this problem. Not only that, but I need to protect myself and my family. I will also press charges if I receive another phone call.

Carla—Did you hear Doris' ultimatum?

SAM—Yes, I did. What you're saying, Doris, is that you won't see me anymore if I don't get her in. And that's just what she wants, you to not see me anymore—so she'll be victorious.

Carla—You're giving her the power. You can stay in therapy, but you will have to leave her or she will have to come in. That's your ultimatum. You need to tell her, "You go in to see Doris with me, or I'm leaving you," or choose to leave therapy.

SAM—Okay. I'll be powerful.

The session continued for another ten minutes while we talked about different things Sam might do to get Rosalie to escalate her anger. Before he left Sam agreed that he would call that night to let us know his wife's decision. Later that night Sam did call and said that his wife had agreed to come in. We arranged a joint session with Rosalie, Sam, Carla, and me.

ACT FIVE

Scene I—Joint session with Sam and wife

From the onset of the session it was very obvious how Sam had set things up for a roaring game of "Let You and Him Fight" between Rosalie and me. The first clue came when Rosalie was introduced to Carla. Rosalie responded in an angry tone, "I didn't even know there was another therapist involved." It seems that Sam had conveniently forgotten to tell Rosalie that another therapist was working with him.

As Rosalie talked, she revealed more clues as to how Sam had fueled her anger and jealousy. She described how day after day Sam would refuse to talk with her and when he did talk it was difficult for her to hear him, as he usually had a newspaper in front of his face. On group night, however, Sam would be noticeably different. He would walk around the house smiling and mumbling to himself about the group and the other members. To fan Rosalie's fantasies even more, Sam would dress unusally nice for the group and would make a point of telling Rosalie how well I always looked. Sam would come home late the night of the group . . . at least several hours after the group was over. He would hint at what a fun time he had had with the group at a local pizza joint. He failed to mention that I didn't go with the group.

During the session Rosalie also became aware of how Sam had been setting things up for her to be angry with me. As her awareness of what Sam had been doing increased, her anger toward me was somewhat dissipated. She was then able to give both Carla and me added information as to how Sam's behavior had changed since he had entered group. She said that Sam had consistently left notes lying around the house . . . notes that he had obviously wanted her to read. She recalled that one was entitled, "Reasons I Should Leave My Wife"; while another was entitled, "What I Would Do Differently If I Were Not Married." Since Sam's behavior toward her had become more negative since he had been attending group, Rosalie had come to the conclusion that it was *that Doris*, his therapist, who was causing him to behave in such a way.

Rosalie had played into the game by not calling me and making an appointment to talk about what was going on. Then each week she would get madder and madder at me. Worst of all, by doing this she was also acting out her husband's anger. Sam had been angry with his wife for years, and had been angry with Carla and me and the group because we had not been buying his "nice guy" role. By concentrating on Sam's behavior in the present, Rosalie was able to discount that the marriage had been bad for many years. She wanted to think that if Sam would just get away from *that Doris*, everything would be fine.

During the session with Rosalie and Sam, Carla and I constantly confronted Sam's grins and "innocent" little boy remarks that incited Rosalie. At the end of the session both Carla and I recommended that Rosalie and Sam see us conjointly so things could be dealt with in the open. Using her anger with me as an excuse to avoid therapy, Rosalie refused to come in; however, she did agree to stop all harassing phone calls.

Scene II—Next group therapy session with Sam

We asked Sam to report to the group what had been going on and also to report about the joint session he had had with his wife, Carla, and me. Sam did report what had gone on, but denied the seriousness of the situation by the way he presented the information. I told Sam that he needed to take responsibility for helping to set up his wife to act out his anger. I then told him that he needed to run out four ways he had been provoking Rosalie.

Sam fiddled and fooled around as he had in previous sessions. He told us that we were really making *too much* out of the whole situation. It was at this time that I decided that if Sam refused to see the seriousness of the situation, I would refuse to be his therapist. None of us knew what Rosalie might do if he kept provoking her. He laughed and said I was exaggerating what Rosalie might do. I said that I was not exaggerating and furthermore because he was minimizing the seriousness of the situation, I was not willing, nor was Carla willing, to see him any longer in therapy.

Carla told Sam that his behavior scared her. She supported what I had said and then I told Sam that he had the rest of the group time to decide whether to get in his Adult and tell the group four ways he had been provoking his wife or whether he would stay in his Child and test us to see if we meant what we said. Forty minutes later group time was up and Sam had still not reported to the group. I then told Sam that he had made the decision. I was terminating his therapy with us. Tonight was his last session.

Scene III—*The next group therapy session.*

The group discussed what had gone on with Sam the week before. People in the group expressed a variety of feelings. All expressed relief that I had terminated Sam because they could see that he wanted his wife to do something violent. They were glad that we were protecting ourselves. Most of the members said that they felt sad and scared that Sam would choose to play such a dangerous game. Some felt angry that Sam was discounting at such a high level and that he refused to see the danger of the situation.

Both Carla and I felt a mixture of feelings. We expressed fear that Sam's wife would hurt someone or hurt herself. We both felt glad that we had protected ourselves. I made one point very clear, and that was that I would not care about Sam's problem and whether or not he solved his problem more than he cared himself. I would not be a Rescuer and then be a Victim of him and his wife's persecutions.

EPILOGUE

Several days after our terminating Sam's treatment, a very scared Rosalie called and asked if I would take her husband back in treatment. I refused to do this. I had decided that I had done all I could do. I had exposed their dangerous game and had given them a lot of information. If I took him back, there were too many risks involved, as well as too many feelings to work through before they would be able to work on the real problem. I did refer them to another therapist and strongly urged that they have conjoint therapy. Both did agree to do that. Several months later as I was shopping, I saw them together at a store. They made a point of coming over and telling me that things were going well for them. They also thanked me for sending them to another therapist who was continuing to work with them.

IV

AS THE WORLD TURNS

No matter how insistent or how often people say that they wish to solve their problems, the actual therapeutic process is slow and hard work, because people are resistant to change. For example, a man gets information from his wife that his passivity is interfering with their marriage, and that unless he changes she will leave him. He may understand that he needs to converse more with his wife; take a more active part in parenting the children; and be more involved with planning the social calendar, handling the money, and structuring family time. He understands that these expectations are appropriate. He also knows in his Adult ego state that when he makes these changes he will be a happier and healthier person. He may, therefore, wants to do all these new behaviors, but to change after thirty years is difficult. His old behavior is much more comfortable. Learning new behaviors is scary, so he will resist giving up the old, comfortable ways.

In this chapter I am presenting a week-by-week account of what went on with three different people—Janet, Eric, and Albert. These transcripts will show several ways each individual resists solving his/her particular problems. When one way of resistance is confronted, each quickly finds another way to resist change.

There are several ways a person can avoid changing. One

way to avoid working on a problem is to bring up another problem which seems more immediate than the initial one. Then the person works on the more immediate problem, thereby avoiding working through the more critical one. For example, in the first transcript Janet talks about the game she had played with the group the previous week. Although this is an important issue that she needs to deal with, Janet conveniently ignores the issue that she had brought up the previous week—her boyfriend's inability to have an erection. Another group member questions Janet about her discounting important information and not dealing with the real issue. It was then that I noticed that Janet was always working, but was seldom solving any problem because she was constantly switching from problem to problem. After becoming aware of Janet's maneuvering, I realized that there were others who were avoiding change in the same kind of way.

Another reason that change is slow and hard work is that the same problem may manifest itself on many different levels. A person may work through an issue on one level, but the problem may reappear in other forms or on other levels. An example of this is the man who is having trouble getting along with his wife. In therapy he states that he is angry because "my wife is always telling me what to do." Then he realizes that because he doesn't make decisions his wife makes decisions for both of them. In group he works on his problem of not making decisions in their marriage. After several weeks it becomes clear that he is constantly wanting others in the group to tell him what to do. After being confronted each time he asks the group to make his decisions for him, and stroked when he himself makes a decision, he starts to come through for himself in the group. He also transfers this behavior to his marriage. He reports that both he and his wife are pleased at his new assertiveness, and he no longer feels like a little boy in the relationship. Several months later he comes to group and talks about how unhappy he has become at work. After discussing this in group, it becomes evident that he is now acting like a little boy at work and wants his boss to make all the decisions. He is holding onto the "little boy" position and succeeding in transferring his dependency from his wife and the group onto his boss.

In this chapter, "As The World Turns," you will see how Janet, Eric, and Albert start to work on their problems, resist solving them, overcome their resistance, and eventually solve the problem.

JANET

(Sex, Competition, and Other Dirty Words)

Week I

JANET—I'll work. I want to talk about the game I played in group last week. What I figured out over the week is that I played "Social Rapo."[20] What I did was come to the group two weeks ago and say that I wanted information about Ron spending weekends at my apartment. I was concerned at the time about how it might affect the kids, and also what the neighbors would think. Also, what would I say if my folks called some Saturday morning about 8:00 A.M. and Ron answered—how would I explain why he was at my house so early? What I figured out with the group's help was that I was taking responsibility for my parents' feelings and the neighbors' feelings. When I left group I felt resolved and told everyone I had decided that it was okay for Ron and me to spend the weekend together.

Then last week I came in here angry and told the group that I was going to continue to be responsible for my parents' feelings and not let Ron spend the weekends. If they found out, or rather if my father found out, it would kill him. I had already messed up once by marrying a bum. And I'm sure he would consider Ron a bum if he knew we were sleeping together before we got married. The way I played Social Rapo was to say one week that I was resolved and felt good about the decision to let Ron stay with me on weekends, and then I came in mad the next week, as though it was you who had told me what to do.

Doris—Right. You got information and support to make your *own* decision and then you got mad at us for the decision you made. You pulled a switch.

JANET—Yes, and I apologize. I am now making the decision that I am not going to allow him to spend the weekends at my house.

GUS—What I'm wondering about is that last week you told us that Ron has trouble having erections, and that being able to go to bed with him when you both wanted to was a way to help him with his problem. So your decision doesn't make sense to me.

JANET—Yes . . . but since we will be married in a month, I think we can work on it after our marriage. What I did do, however, was to talk to Ron the other night about his inability to have an erection lately. He was mad and scared when I told him that I had told the group about his problem. He then asked me if Lori, a friend of mine knew. I said, "Yes," and that made him even more angry at me, and also at Lori because she knew. He told me that he did not *under any circumstances* want me to talk to Lori about the issue again. I agreed. I made a complete commitment. But the next morning I got up, went to work, and felt really scared. As the day progressed, I got more scared. Later I couldn't stand how I felt, so I called Lori and told her what had happened.

Carla—Okay. You're saying you were scared, but what you did was an angry thing.

JANET—Yeah. I gave Ron a firm commitment that I was not going to run the issue out to Lori; but I called the next morning and ran it out to her.

Doris—I want to check something out. What game have you been playing with Ron and Lori?

JANET—Well, Social Rapo for one. I promised *not* to tell Lori about the discussion Ron and I had, and then I told Lori. And also I've been playing "Two Against One."

Doris—Okay, Janet, what's the *real issue* that you need to work on?

JANET—I don't know what you're getting at.

Doris—Well, what I'm getting at is that last week you told us that Ron was having trouble having an erection, and when you first talked with him about it he had a grin on his face, and you got scared. Rightly so. That grin said that there must be some advantage for him not to have an erection. Then in here you agreed to talk with Ron about the problem and his smiling. Instead of dealing with *that* issue you are creating a whole new problem around who told who what. So I think that this is a way to avoid the real issue that you and Ron need to deal with before you get married. You have already been married to one guy who didn't come through.

JANET—So Marshall didn't come through financially and now Ron many not come through sexually. I see . . . Okay. The real issue is Ron not having an erection lately, and what is he going to do about it, and how will I deal with it.

Doris—Right.

JANET—Okay. I know the problem is not a medical one. I also know that when we are fighting with each other . . . that's when he has trouble. So I get bitchy and then he can't have an erection . . . No, he *won't* get an erection. So if he chooses to deal with his anger in that way, I will choose not to marry him. I will give him the information tonight after the group.

Doris—Okay.

JANET—One other thing. I want to make a contract with the group to report back each week as to how the erection is doing [group laughter]. As to whether or not Ron's having an erection.

Doris—Okay. Good.

Week II

JANET—I know there's not much time left tonight, but I'd like to report on what's been going on with me and Ron. We've been sleeping together this week and he has had an erection every time.

Doris—No trouble?

JANET—No trouble whatever! We have had a lot of good talks and have exchanged a whole lot of information, and if Ron has the problem again, he has agreed to come and talk about it with you, Doris.

Carla—That's good, Janet. I'm glad. I am wondering what you've done about letting Ron spend the weekends at your house.

JANET—Well . . . a . . . he did spend the weekend this past week, but he won't anymore.

ROBBIE—Last time you told us that you had decided not to let him stay with you. Now you've changed it again. You've played "Social Rapo" with us again.

JANET—I didn't want my parents to know.

ROBBIE—What does that have to do with us?

JANET—Well . . . I guess nothing.

ROBBIE—So why bring your parents in this room? I'm talking about your not telling us you had changed your mind. We're not your parents. We already told you that you were a big girl and could make your own decisions about Ron's sleeping at your house. I feel angry that you discounted our support.

JANET—I'm sorry. I did discount. I keep bringing my parents' values in here. I want to please you, and I think the way to do that is not to have Ron sleep at my house.

GUS—Well, please stop doing that. I don't like you assuming that I think you're a bad girl if you sleep with Ron. I personally thought it was smart of you two to work on Ron's problem of not having an erection before you got married.

JANET—Okay. I hear you.

Doris—Now that you've heard . . . what does that mean in terms of Ron sleeping at your house?

JANET—I won't make a decision about Ron's not sleeping at my house.

Doris—And what does that mean?

JANET—A . . . well, I will say that I still feel bad if he sleeps over when I think about how my father would react if he knew. Otherwise, I feel okay about it.

Doris—You're still not saying what that means.

JANET—Oh, hell, I will let Ron sleep over, and I'm not going to worry about it. We are old enough to decide for ourselves what we want to do.

Carla—I'd like to be sure your Adult is on in this decision. So give us three reasons why you will let Ron sleep over.

JANET—Okay. One reason is because Ron is more likely to be able to work through his problem if we allow ourselves to have sex spontaneously, instead of knowing that Tuesday night is the night because we're at his apartment. Another reason is because I like it [laughter]. I like having him at my house. Also, I know that we are not doing anything wrong. We are going to be married, and we love each other.

Carla—Those sound like good reasons to me, Janet. Remember them when you start fighting the Parent in your head or start switching on the group. Those are your reasons and you made the decision.

JANET—Right.

Doris—Okay. Group's over. See you all next week.

Week III

JANET—I'll work. I want to tell everybody that this week our sexual relationship has been beautiful. I'm really happy and hopeful about all of it.

Doris—Good. I like the way you have been sticking to your contract each week.

JANET—Thanks. Now I'd like to talk about one more thing. The boys, my sons, we're having an issue about bedtime. They never want to go to bed. It seems that right at bedtime they have the most energy. It's been quite a hassle getting them to bed. What Ron and I decided is that we will put them to bed and give them a ten-minute period of messing around after they go to bed. We set the timer for ten minutes. During that time they can talk, laugh, play, get into each other's beds, or whatever they want to do; but when the ten minutes are up and the bell rings, we come in to say goodnight.

JEFFREY—Is that method working, Janet?

JANET—Yes. And if the boys don't settle down after we tuck them in, then there are consequences. And it's working.

Doris—I have to say that even though it's working right now, I don't think it's a good solution for the boys. They go to bed, you allow them to get highly stimulated, and then they have to be quiet when the timer goes off. There's no transition period where they have time to settle down.

JANET—I hear you Doris, but our method is working.

GUS—I'm wondering if this issue is another way to set it up to mess up your sex life? Hassling with kids at bedtime takes a lot of energy.

JANET—I'll have to think about that. Another thing, because Ron has never had kids and was an only child himself, we both think it would be a good idea if we got more information on parenting the boys. So I'd like to set up a joint session for next week, Doris.

Doris—That's fine with me.

JANET—Good. I'll make the appointment with you after group tonight.

Week IV

JANET—I want to tell the group that this week Ron and I had sex and it was fine. I think that a lot of that was due to the information we got in our joint session with Doris. It was really helpful.

One of the things Ron and I discovered was that the children have been a distraction in terms of our sex life. Doris explained to us how the boys would naturally feel competitive with Ron, a new man on the scene, when for five years they have been the only "men" in my life. So one way they would have of expressing this jealousy would be to hassle us at a time when the two of us wanted to be alone. I played into this situation by feeling guilty about bringing Ron into the house. I also didn't want to be firm because I wanted us to all get along. I wanted the boys to like their new Daddy-to-be. Ron played into the situation by trying to win the boys' affection. He was afraid to be firm for fear they wouldn't like him. We were allowing the boys to win the competition against Ron because we were often very tired after hassling with the boys. Truthfully, we were too tired for sex. I guess we have to also admit that *we* were using the boys to sabotage our sex life. So I think you were right, Doris, that our bedtime solution was not a good one.

JEFFREY—So what are you going to do differently?

JANET—It may sound strange, but since we've gotten this information from Doris, we haven't had the problem. We are firm, and the boys know we mean business.

Another thing we discovered was about Kevin, my six year old, who is competitve with his brother also. He is always saying to his brother, "Let's race!" . . . Or, "I bet I can beat you in Indian wrestling." The problem here is that Kevin wins all the time and his brother loses; and what we had been doing was not praising Kevin for winning, or only praising him a little.

ROBBIE—How old is his brother?

JANET—Chris is ten months older, but they are both about the same size. What Doris said was that it is normal for a six-year-old to want to compete. That's one of the ways a six-year-old gets some of his okay feelings. What we also learned is that Chris was getting lots of strokes for losing, while Kevin got only a minimal amount of strokes for winning. When it looked as though Kevin would win, Chris would give up. He would just quit. So Kevin would finish the race, and instead of getting lots of strokes for winning, he didn't get many, because I didn't want to hurt Chris' feelings. So in this way we were stroking Chris to lose and also giving Kevin a message, "If you lose, you get more strokes." So this week, Ron and I have been giving strokes to Kevin for winning.

Carla—That's good information you ran out.

Doris—You really did hear what we talked about.

JEFFREY—You do persist in getting the job done. I like the way you work and take care of your problems.

Week V

JANET—I want to work. First I want to report that I've seen Ron a lot this week and things are really good sexually, no problems at all. Second, I want to report that since we've been stroking Kevin for winning, Chris has begun to try harder. The other day Chris even won a race. We stroke both of the boys for doing a good job so both boys feel good.

GUS—Wow! That's great.

JEFFREY—I think so, too. It's taking away from the winning and losing aspect, and I think that's neat.

ROBBIE—So do I.

JANET—Thanks. Now I want to talk about another problem that I'm having with my boys. The problem is the dirty words that they are starting to say. What Ron and I tell them is that people will not like you. What people will do is judge you by hearing you say dirty words, and that's why we don't want you to say them. The problem is that Ron and I cuss sometimes. So how can I tell my kids not to say dirty words with Mommy running around saying them? A big double message. As I see it, I have two choices. Either I can stop and Ron can stop, or we can all swear.

Doris—Well, what's another option?

JANET—We could all say them when nobody else was around.

Doris—Another option?

JANET—I don't know another option.

Doris—Oh, yeah, there's others.

JANET—Well, I can't think of any other options.

Doris—Okay. What I would like you to do is to go home and write down all the options. What can you do about your kids saying dirty words?

JANET—Okay. I'm fine with that suggestion. Is it okay to get Ron to help me think of options?

Doris—Is it?

JANET—Yes. We share the problem.

The following week Janet came back and reported that she and Ron had decided that even though they themselves both swear, it was not good for the boys to cuss, because they were not yet old enough to evaluate when cussing would be inappropriate. Janet continued to work on issues with her boys and on her relationship with Ron. Several months later Janet graduated from the group.

❖❖❖❖❖❖❖❖❖❖❖❖❖❖❖❖❖❖❖❖❖❖❖❖

If one were to lay out all of the problems that one has encountered in one's lifetime on a big sheet of paper, I am convinced of one thing—one would see that most of these problems would stem from a particular pattern of behavior. This pattern of behavior is a result of either a traumatic event in early childhood or repeated childhood experiences which crystallized a person's decision about life and how to behave.

An example of a traumatic experience is one that Dana had. Dana was very close to her Daddy. Her favorite time of day was when Daddy would come home from work and sweep her up in his arms and play with her. When Dana was five years old, Daddy didn't come home one day. She waited and waited and then asked her Mommy, "When is Daddy coming home?" Mommy replied, "Never; your Daddy doesn't love us anymore." Dana's parents got a divorce and Dana never saw Daddy again. The decision that Dana made was: "Men will love you and then leave you." When Dana was seventeen she fell in love with Jim, who asked her to marry him. Before they were married Dana became pregnant. When she told Jim he became angry and accused her of trying to trap him. There was a scene, and then Jim left town, just as Daddy had left her twelve years before. Three years later Dana repeated the same pattern. She fell in love with Andy and became pregnant before marriage. Andy was drafted before they were married and never came back to her, though he kept writing and saying that they would get married. Thus, Dana continued to set up her life experiences which reenacted the early traumatic event of Daddy leaving.

An example of repeated childhood experience is what happened with Keith. Keith recalls that when he was three years of age, he was bringing his Mommy a box of soap powder. He dropped it and spilled it all over the kitchen floor. Mommy reacted by screaming, "Every time I ask you to do something you mess it up." Keith can remember the same kind of scene happening over and over, always with his Mommy saying. "Every time I ask you to do something you mess it up." Keith's decision was, "I can never please women; I will mess up with women." In therapy Keith realized how he had proven this out with women school teachers. When he had female teachers in grade school, high school, or college, he was lucky to make a C. When he had a male teacher, he would make an A. He also was unable to maintain any personal relationship with a woman for any length of time. He would eventually do something to mess up the relationship.

In these two ways we can see how a person makes certain decisions early in life. From these decisions a particular pattern of behavior develops which the person then tends to follow for the rest of his/her life. At first one's problems may appear insurmountable; however, once a person sees the particular pattern of behavior which has manifested itself in many different disguises, he can see that he has an option to change the pattern. In order to change a behavior a person has to make a new decision, decide to change the behavior which reinforced the old decision, and follow up with behavior appropriate to the new decision. Making a new decision is ineffective if one does not also develop a plan of action to follow.

In this next transcript, we can see that Eric's first decision was, "I'm not going to grow up." All his adult life he had figured out various ways to get people to take care of him so he could remain a little boy. In the following excerpts he talks about not being able to find a job, being depressed, and problems with his wife and mother. All of these issues resulted from the decision he had made in childhood not to grow up.

While in therapy Eric made a redecision to grow up. It was soon evident to Eric and to the group, that he was not certain that this new decision was a good one. Eric found that it was a struggle to change old ways of behavior.

ERIC

(I Won't Grow Up)

Week I

ERIC—I'd like to work. I want to bring the group up to date on what's been going on with me. One of the things that I'm most concerned with now is my job situation. I still have not been able to find a job.

STEVE—How long have you been out of work?

ERIC—For three months. It's funny, but I think the reason that I can't find a job is that I'm overqualified. I thought I had something all wound up, but it fell through at the last minute. But I'm certainly looking, so perhaps by next week . . .

CLIFFORD—What kind of job are you looking for, Eric?

ERIC—Something to do with management—either as a consultant or some administrative position. Since I have my doctorate in business administration, I think I would like to do something with developing a business or being a consultant for small businesses.

SUE—Do you have any leads?

Eric—No. The problem is that I'd hoped to be able to tell my parents that I had a new job. We stayed with them last week and it was very difficult to avoid answering their questions about my having a job.

Doris—Why did you want to avoid dealing with the job issue with them, Eric?

Eric—Because I've given them hints that I was going to be changing jobs and didn't tell them that I'd been fired. How does one tell one's parents that he has been fired from his position of Vice President at a large company? I just couldn't do it.

Doris—Why not?

Eric—I figured they would be very anxious and concerned about my being fired and not having another job.

Doris—Well, what actually did happen when you went home? You said that they already had some hints.

Eric—Well, my mother didn't say anything directly to me; but she did question my wife, Liz, very closely. My mom's very good at reading between the lines and I myself am not very good at faking it.

Doris—Okay. Let's say that you told your parents directly, "I don't have a job." How would your parents feel?

Eric—They would feel sad.

Doris—They would feel sad. And then what would they do?

Eric—They would start giving me advice about getting another job. It wouldn't be critical advice. It would be very supportive. They are really into taking care of their children . . . even though this child is forty-four years old.

Doris—Would they do anything else?

Eric—Probably press money on me. And then I would feel like a dependent child.

Doris—Well, what did happen when you went home?

Eric—They did get concerned and they did give us money. It was like they knew, but they didn't know.

Doris—You're starting to whistle under your breath, Eric. Why are you whistling?

ERIC—Probably Rebellious Child. That's been the feedback before.

Doris—Rebellious kids rebel against something or someone. So who are you rebelling against?

ERIC—Against? I guess I'm rebelling against being dependent. I'm rebelling against being dependent on my parents. You see, my mom is a very strong woman. She has always had to take care of the family. My father hasn't been able to work for the last thirty years. When I was a teenager, he fell off a ladder and broke his back, and as a result he hasn't been able to work. He collects money for his disability. Mom has always been the one to take care of things. Now she's getting older and she looks tired. I spent a lot of time while I was there nagging her and telling her how she should get a washer and dryer and she should get air conditioning and this and that. She always says, "No, no I don't need that stuff." I realized that my nagging wasn't helping her at all. She's not willing to change things. She's not willing to have someone or something take care of her or make her life easier. She's still the parent, unwilling to be dependent. And me, I've been dependent all my life. I'm trying to reverse roles, and it just doesn't work.

Doris—And how did you perpetuate your being a child this weekend?

ERIC—By not being straight about my job situation. By not telling her what was going on in my life.

Carla—So your behavior this past week tells us that you actually set it up to continue the rebellion.

Doris—You're starting to whistle again, Eric.

ERIC—I wasn't aware of it. Yeah . . . okay, I was whistling.

Doris—So I'm thinking that you whistle when we start to get close to the *real* issue, which is that you like being dependent. In fact, you set it up to be dependent. And when we talk about it or start to confront you, you get rebellious and start to whistle.

Carla—And had you been straight with your folks, what would have happened is that they would have offered you money, and you would have had to take responsibility to tell them "yes" or "no." This would have meant that you were grown-up.

Eric—I guess I do like being dependent in some ways, but I know that that is what my mother really wants too.

Carla—It sounds like it from what you told us tonight.

Doris—The other thing I want to check out is that when you're dependent on them, how are you feeling?

Eric—Angry, very angry at myself and them.

Doris—And how are you expressing that anger?

Eric—I mostly suppress it. Once in a while it pops out at Liz and the kids, but usually I suppress it.

Doris—And when you suppress your anger, what happens?

Eric—I get depressed.

Doris—So what you're doing is perpetuating your script. You're depressed and you're not growing up. Two big script messages; "Be Depressed," and "Don't Grow Up."

Eric—I do understand what I'm doing. I'm choosing to stay in a dependent situation with my folks and then I can feel depressed.

Week II

Eric—I want to work this week on the issue we talked about last week; my not growing up and my being depressed. I thought about it a lot. I know that in spite of my having a doctorate degree I am keeping myself a little boy, even with my wife and kids. I want you to know that I can really see it. This week I made a new decision—I'm going to grow up!

GROUP—Wow! That's great! Neat!

ERIC—I also thought about the whistling. I caught myself whistling several times this week. Once when I was with my kids. They were fighting and I caught myself whistling. I realized that I was whistling to avoid being the Daddy and stopping the fighting. By whistling and saying nothing I was being a powerless little boy. And the other time . . .

Doris—Wait, Eric. I want to stop you. What did you do when you realized what your whistling was about?

ERIC—Well, I became powerful and made the kids stop fighting.

Doris—I want you to claim that behavior, Eric. You did an important thing for yourself and the kids.

Carla—I agree. That's also how you keep yourself from getting strokes for good things you do. You don't tell us how you solve the problem; then people don't get to stroke you and help reinforce your new decision to grow up. It's also a way to stay depressed—if there's no reward for changing, why change?

ERIC—I see that . . . hmm . . . I'd like for the group to tell me I did a good job.

GROUP—[Strokes Eric.]

ERIC—Well, here's another one [laughter]. I caught myself whistling the other day when Liz and I were talking about where we were going on vacation. When I caught myself whistling, I said to myself, "Okay, what's going on? What aren't you dealing with?" I then realized I was mad at her because she was telling me where we were going and what we were going to do, instead of discussing it with me. So I told Liz I was mad, and that we were going to negotiate the plans.

GROUP—Wow! Is that neat!

STEVE—I'll say. Then what happened, Eric?

ERIC—Well, we sat down and talked for over an hour. We ended up compromising. We're both going to have our way.

We're going to spend one week in Boston doing sightseeing and one week camping.

Doris—I feel really good when I see you being assertive and letting yourself make decisions.

ERIC—So do I. Funny, I haven't been depressed all week.

Doris—Could it be there's a connection?

ERIC—Yeah, I know there is.

SEVERAL WEEKS LATER

Week V

Doris—Eric, what's going on with you and Liz? I haven't heard you talk much about your relationship lately. About a month and a half ago you two were really having problems.

ERIC—Right now everything is fine.

Carla—Did you and Liz have a joint session with Doris? I remember you said you wanted one.

ERIC—No. We haven't all gotten together yet. Liz said that she didn't want a joint session. And so we didn't set one up.

Carla—Why did she decide that she didn't want a joint session, Eric?

ERIC—Liz didn't really explain it. She said she felt she didn't need it. That she was doing fine in her group with Doris and didn't need a joint session with the three of us.

Doris—Before you went on vacation, you very much wanted a joint session. Why did you go along with that decision?

ERIC—Because I was scared about the whole thing. I knew we needed to get together and work some things out, but I was scared.

Doris—Liz made the decision. You were being a dependent little boy again, giving all the power to Mommy.

Eric—That's not entirely true. I said I wanted the session and, well, she kept postponing it. She kept putting it off. I confronted Liz on the importance of the session at two or three different times, and it seemed to be a very low priority for her.

Doris—And what do you want *for you*?

Eric—I completely suppressed what I wanted until Carla brought it up. It's still very threatening to get together for a joint session.

Doris—That doesn't answer my question.

Eric—What do I want for me? Well, I don't think I want a joint session.

Carla—So what are you going to do with all the information you got from Doris about the relationship that you and Liz have?

Eric—I'm denying it.

Doris—You're whistling, Eric.

Eric—I'll deny the information until there is a crisis.

Sis—I feel sad you're doing that.

Doris—How have you been feeling this last month, Eric?

Eric—Generally pretty good, except for not being able to get a job.

Doris—How many days of depression have you had this last month?

Eric—Very few.

Doris—Are they on the increase again?

Eric—No. When I get depressed, I have ways of getting out of it.

Doris—What do you do to get out of it?

Eric—Just start new things, talk to new people, just get active.

Doris—What I'm concerned about is that you're going to start being depressed again, because you're setting up your life to have that happen. You're again letting Liz make all the decisions and giving her all the power. Also, you're waiting for a crisis.

GAIL—I'm bothered that you're once again sitting on all the information that you have.

Carla—What was the information, Eric?

ERIC—That Liz wants me in a powerless position. And when I start feeling good and not depressed and saying what I want in our relationship, that's when she starts to think about getting a divorce.

Doris—And what it looks like to me is that you are starting to give up your power instead of dealing with the issues about what Liz will do if you grow up and start taking care of yourself. So you are choosing to remain in a symbiotic relationship;[21] a relationship where you must stay weak and Liz must stay strong for the relationship to survive. And if you threaten to change your position in the relationship and become stronger, Liz threatens to end the relationship.

ERIC—That is right. Okay. I got some really good information tonight. Thanks.

Doris—All right. I'd like you to report back next week on the information you got, both this week and several weeks ago. I think what goes on with your parents and what goes on with Liz is very much related.

Week VI

ERIC—Okay. Last week, Doris, you asked me to put together information I had about how I relate to my folks and also about how I relate to Liz. So I wrote it down and I want to read it. First, in both my relationships with my parents and with Liz, I am the little boy, the dependent child. Second, both my mother and my wife have an investment in my continuing to be a dependent little boy. Third, when I was a child and tried to assert my independence, my mother withdrew from me. She sulked and acted as though I wasn't being a good son. I remember how excited I was when our scout troop was scheduled to go on an overnight trip, and how she fussed and how I wanted to go so badly, but in the end stayed home because of her. Now Liz, my wife, threatens to leave me if I become independent and say what I want. And fourth, that I have felt angry all these years with my folks and Liz for wanting me to be a little boy, but instead of using my anger to change the situation, what I did was to turn it on myself. Consequently, I have been depressed most of my life.

Doris—Wow! That is really great the way you connected everything up.

Carla—I agree.

STEVE—Really good work, Eric.

ERIC—Thanks.

Doris—One more thing I want to pick up on. And that is, what have you decided to do with all the information you now have?

ERIC—What I'm going to do is to *grow up*, stop being depressed, take charge of my life, stop letting other people run my life for me.

Doris—And how will we know that you are doing all those things, Eric?

ERIC—You'll know because I won't be depressed in order to elicit people's sympathy. I'll be happy. You'll also know that I'm growing up when I stop fooling around about a job and actually get myself one and start working. Also, I will be telling people what I want and what I don't want. I'll be telling Liz.

Carla—You sound very convincing. What will you do when Liz threatens a divorce?

ERIC—I'm going to call her bluff. I know she doesn't really want to leave. I'm going to insist on a joint session.

KATHY—I really like the way you worked in here tonight . . .

putting information together, making good decisions about your life. You really sound powerful.

ERIC—I agree [laughter].

GROUP—[Laughter.]

Week VII

ERIC— I'd like to work. This past week has been a really bad week. It's been the worst week since I've been in the group. And I'm not really sure what's happening, but I've just felt *really* depressed.

Doris—Eric, you said you were feeling depressed, and depressed is not a feeling. It's a state of being. So I would like for you to get in touch with what you've been feeling.

ERIC—Well, scared. I've been sort of scared.

Doris—Because?

ERIC—I'm scared to do things. I don't know if that makes sense. I think I'm scared of being rejected, and also a little scared that I won't do the right thing, make the right decisions. Things like this. The depression is really real.

Doris—I believe you, Eric. What we know is that depression is the symptom, but it's just *that*—a symptom. It usually means there is something else going on.

ERIC—I see.

MICHAEL—Did you and your wife have your joint session?

ERIC—Yes. It went very well and we got a lot of stuff cleared up. One of the big things I found out about me is that I still set it up for Liz to take care of me. Like I withdraw in the evening and expect that she will do something to make me feel better. What was decided was that I would need to ask her directly if I wanted something from her, and she would confront me if I withdrew. So my relationship with Liz is really going better than it has in twelve years.

Doris—So what would be the advantage for you to get depressed *now*, Eric?

ERIC—Um . . . it would be counter-productive. I know that. However, I could use my depression as an excuse for not getting on with finding a job . . . or Liz might Rescue me if I got *really* depressed. I just don't think that's it. I have been actively looking for a job and my relationship with Liz has been much better since our joint session with Doris, and also since I have made a decision to grow up. Also, our son's report card was better than it has been since kindergarten. His behavior has been very good. I spoke with the teacher last week and she said that she was having no discipline problems with Jason. So I should be feeling great . . . not scared.

Doris—One more check out then. Is it okay for you to feel good?

ERIC—Maybe that's the problem. I am scared that if I feel good and grow up I will be abandoned.

Doris—You don't have to feel afraid of being abandoned, because you can take care of yourself now. It's okay to feel good about yourself and to be in control of *your* feelings and *your* life. You're grown-up now.

ERIC—I'm starting to feel better already [laughter].

GROUP—[Laughter.]

Doris—Eric, what things do you do differently in your life when you're feeling good?

ERIC—I'm more alive, more active, have more energy. I'm willing to meet new people and talk to people. Just a lot of things.

Doris—Are those good payoffs for you?

ERIC—Yes, indeed. I was enjoying them and I'm going to start enjoying them again.

Eric continued to work in the group on how he would set himself up to be depressed and how he would wait for his wife to Rescue him. The group would confront Eric's not being assertive and would support him when he made decisions, dealt with his anger, and asked for strokes in a straight way. Eric did find a job and left the city. The night he left the group he reported that he had not been depressed for three months. He had felt angry, but he had expressed his anger; he had felt sad, but he had asked for strokes. He was pleased with his job because he was handling his responsibilities and making decisions. The group and Eric felt good because Eric had successfully reversed his earlier decision, "Don't Grow Up," to "It's Okay to Grow Up." He was now able to recognize and stop the old destructive behavior patterns which reinforced his old decision. He had begun to take responsibility for his actions, his feelings, and his life.

In this last transcript I will show how clever Albert is at finding ways to keep from losing weight. He had come for therapy because he wanted to lose weight, wanted to improve his relationship with others, and wanted to make his own decisions. The main way Albert keeps from getting anywhere is to play the game of "Corner."[22] No matter what anyone does, Albert gets to be madder and madder. The madder he gets, the more he can eat and the more he can eat, the fatter he gets. The fatter he gets the madder he is, the more he can eat. Sound like a game? It surely is!

ALBERT

(Standing In The Corner Watching All the Weight Piling Up)

Week I

ALBERT—I'd like to work. Last week when we left group I got to thinking about what happened. I had confronted Carol about always using TA words and she got defensive. She told me that it was okay for her to use TA words because the group did use TA. Then Carla said that my confrontation was right on and I think that was a Rescue. I'm mad at you, Carla, because I don't need you to Rescue me. I think you discount me taking care of myself.

Carla—What did you want me to do, Albert?

ALBERT—Well, not Rescue me.

Carla—That's what you don't want. What do you want?

ALBERT—I don't know.

Doris—Carla gave you support for your confrontation of Carol . . . and you got mad. Carla did not Rescue you. How would you have felt if Carla had said nothing in support of your confrontation?

ALBERT—Probably mad.

Doris—Probably?

ALBERT—Yeah . . . I would have been mad at the fact that other people didn't support me.

Doris—So either way, Albert, we are in a corner. If we support you, you get mad and if we don't support you, you get mad.

ALBERT—I see that.

Doris—So what are the advantages of getting mad?

ALBERT—I don't know.

Doris—Well, let's think about it. You get mad; then what do you do?

ALBERT—I usually get quiet, withdrawn.

Doris—Or?

ALBERT—Sometimes I talk to my wife about the problems and then she gives me a back rub or fixes me something to eat. Then I feel better.

Doris—So she Rescues you with a back rub or food when you are mad.

ALBERT—Yeah. I guess you could say she Rescues me.

Doris—You guess?

ALBERT—Sometimes it's support that she gives. Like when I feel tired after work. Other times it's a Rescue. I don't tell her what's going on and she picks up that I'm depressed and she goes to town.

Doris—What do you mean "goes to town?"

ALBERT—She starts doing things to make me feel better.

Doris—Anybody else Rescue you when you feel bad?

ALBERT—Well, sometimes my uncle and I get into it about our business and after a big blow up, I usually go to my office and close the door. And in about an hour or so my uncle comes in and apologizes.

Doris—And then what happens?

ALBERT—Then we usually take the rest of the day off. We go for a drink or out for a big lunch. Then things are smooth again for awhile.

Doris—Um hmm . . . so what happened last week?

ALBERT—What do you mean?

Doris—Well, you left group mad. You were mad at Carla because she supported you. What did you do after you left.

ALBERT—I went home.

Doris—And?

ALBERT—Well, my wife and I talked. Oh yeah . . . we also had a sundae. I stopped and got us a sundae at the Velvet Freeze.

Doris—See any pattern in your behavior?

ALBERT—Yeah . . . like every time I get mad, I get to eat.

Doris—Right. You get mad and somebody Rescues you. Your uncle, your wife, or yourself. And most of those Rescues are food Rescues.

ALBERT—So how do I stop getting people to Rescue me with food?

Doris—How do you set the situation up so you will need a Rescuer?

ALBERT—Well, I get mad. No matter what happens, I get mad. And then I start to sulk, so I'm a Victim. And Victims need Rescuers.

Doris—Right on, Albert. So how do you stop getting people to Rescue you with food?

ALBERT—Well . . . I can stop being a Victim so I don't need a Rescuer, or I can make a decision to stop figuring out crooked ways to get food. I did make a contract in here to lose weight and I still haven't lost any.

Doris—How much do you weigh?

ALBERT—About 280. Right now I'm about a hundred pounds overweight.

Doris—You're smiling, Albert. What's the smile about?

ALBERT—I don't know. I need time to think about it.

Doris—Okay. So for next week, I'd like you to get in touch with why you smile when you say that you're a hundred pounds overweight.

ALBERT—Okay.

Week II

ALBERT—I want to work. I was to figure out why I smiled when I said I was a hundred pounds overweight. I figured out what the smile was about. I'm *actually glad* that I'm a hundred pounds overweight. At least part of me is glad. Being fat has been a way for me to be different from other people. When I was a kid I was always like the runt in school. So I started eating and I got heavier, and consequently I got larger; and then people started noticing me more. I have a cousin who is crippled. Because we are the same age, our folks used to visit back and forth a lot. I played a lot with Ben. We also went to the same school. And he got lots of attention for being different. That really sticks in my mind. The weight makes me different too.

Doris—And being different gives you what?

ALBERT—It gives me power. If you're *not different*, then nobody notices you.

Doris—That certainly was true with you and your cousin.

ALBERT—The thing that I know about my weight is that it's also crippling. In a way, it also makes me a cripple.

JEAN—What else happens if you're different and you're a cripple?

ALBERT—If I'm different, people notice me, and if I'm a cripple they take care of me. People are always coming to me and saying, "Boy, you should lose some weight. It will be healthy for you." However, if I give up the weight, I have to have something to replace it. I know that.

Doris—So what could you replace your fat with?

ALBERT—Well . . . taking care of myself more. Last time, last year when I started losing weight, I bought a motorcycle. That worked great for awhile, then I gained weight again.

Doris—Why do you think that happened?

ALBERT—I'm not sure. I think the newness wore off, you know? The motorcycle wasn't the magical solution.

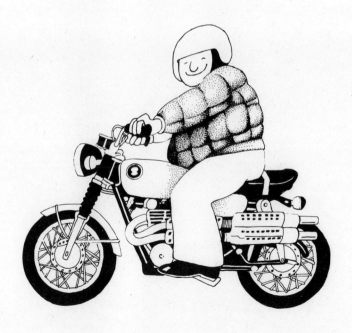

Doris—How many strokes do you think you got from the motor-cycle, Albert?

ALBERT—Oh, lots. I really did—I still love that thing. I ride that damn thing every night.

Doris—I'm glad you enjoy riding, but the pleasure you're getting from the cycle doesn't seem to be enough to replace the food strokes you give yourself.

ALBERT—Well, I joined a bowling team last Sunday. And I'm going hunting this fall for a few days with some friends. We are going to drive to Montana and go after elk. I've never hunted elk before. So I'll get strokes there.

BARB—Do you feel taken care of when you ride your cycle or go hunting?

ALBERT—Yeah . . . that cycle is really something!

Doris—Do you get strokes from *people* when you go riding?

ALBERT—Not always, no . . . Umm . . .

Doris—Okay. Think about what you've told us tonight. Your weight makes you stand out. . . makes you different. You get strokes for being different from other people. If you lose weight, you give up those strokes. And when people give up something, they have to replace that something with something else. Your cycle gives you lots of pleasure, but not enough to replace those strokes. The cycle is a machine. Those strokes about being different came from people.

ALBERT—So you're trying to tell me I need some strokes from people.

Doris—Yes, and I want you to think about it.

ALBERT—Okay, I'll talk about it more next week.

Week III

ALBERT—There's something I figured out that I want from this group, and that is that I want people to confront me more.

I think that I get by with using too many cop-out words like *try* and *perhaps* and *maybe*. And I feel angry that people in here don't pick them up.

Doris—Here we go. I think that you are playing Corner with us, Albert. You're mad because we don't confront you on your use of cop-out words. But I also know that you get mad when people confront you. So we're damned if we don't confront because you'll be mad, and we're damned if we do confront because you'll be mad. That's your old Corner game again.

ALBERT—I don't think you understand.

Doris—What I understand is that no matter what we do, you'll be mad. Also, I'm wondering why you decided to deal with this issue this week when you were to come back and talk about getting strokes from other people and your weight problem.

ALBERT—Well . . . I decided that I get enough strokes.

CHARLES—How much weight have you lost, Albert?

ALBERT—None.

CHARLES—So maybe you need to reevaluate. You yourself told us you had to replace your weight with something.

ALBERT—Okay, I'll evaluate. But I still think I need more confrontation.

Doris—We're not playing your game, Albert.

Week IV

CHARLES—I've thought a lot about the session last week, Albert. Do you remember how you were confronted on playing Corner?

ALBERT—Yeah.

CHARLES—And then I asked you about losing weight and you said that you hadn't lost any.

ALBERT—Um hmm.

CHARLES—Well, I think your bringing up the issue of our confronting you more was a way not to deal with your weight.

ALBERT—Could be.

Doris—Was it?

ALBERT—Well, I did make a contract to tell people how much weight I lost each week and I haven't done that.

CHARLES—And you haven't lost any weight?

ALBERT—No.

Doris—What do you want to do about your weight problem, Albert?

ALBERT—I want to lose. I really do. You know I was supposed to have been a girl. And if I had been a girl, my name was going to be Susie-Q and if I were a boy it was going to be Bar-B-Que. That was a standing joke. And now I'm ready for the Bar-B-Que. I'm ready for the kill [laughter].

Doris—That's not funny, Albert. But that is what you're doing to yourself. Killing yourself with those extra hundred pounds.

ALBERT—All right. I want to make a contract and keep it. I will lose weight, and each week I'll report back to the group as to how much weight I've lost.

Doris—No deal! You still haven't told us what you're going to replace the weight with.

ALBERT—Okay. By next week I'll have things figured out.

Week V

ALBERT—I want to say that I've been doing a lot of thinking. And what I've decided is that I *do* need strokes *from people*. And if I can get "people strokes," I think I can lose weight. Several years back I went to Weight Watchers and I lost fifteen pounds and I got good strokes. People would clap when I weighed in, so I signed up again for Weight Watchers.

Doris—That's great!

ALBERT—Yeah . . . and I have a goal that I'll lose one hundred pounds. And this time I'm going to do it.

CEIL—I bet you will.

ALBERT—Okay. And every week I'll report on my weight loss. I'll report at Weight Watchers and get good strokes and I'll report here and get good strokes.

Doris—That's really smart.

ALBERT—Also, I want to thank you, Charles, for saying what you did last week. And also you, Doris, and Carla for the way you didn't let me get by with any games.

Carla—Thanks, Albert.

Doris—Ditto. One more thing, I'm still concerned about how you are going to get "people strokes." What are you going to do differently?

ALBERT—Well, I already said that I would get strokes at Weight Watchers and in the group. What I also will do is ask my wife for a back rub each night. I love back rubs! Also, my uncle and I have decided to go to the gym during our lunch hour on Mondays, Wednesdays, and Fridays. I'll get in shape and give myself lots of strokes for doing that. I enjoy my uncle's company and I will ask him for strokes too.

Doris—I really like those ways you are going to get strokes. I would also like for you to think of five other ways that you can get strokes that don't have anything to do with eating or weight.

ALBERT—Like spending money on myself?

Doris—That's a good start.

ALBERT—I think I'm going to like this contract. Okay. Next week I'll bring in five ways that I can get strokes from other people that have nothing to do with eating or weight.

Carla—Good.

GROUP—Good work, Albert. I really believe you'll do it this time . . . wonderful!

Albert has continued to work in the group and at the writing of this book, he has lost fifty pounds. He has replaced his food strokes with lots of "people strokes." He continues to be an active group member. He has stopped setting it up for people to be mad at him for playing Corner, and therefore he gets positive strokes instead of the negative strokes he was getting. He admits that he has a lot of work to do, but feels good about the insights and the progress he has made so far.

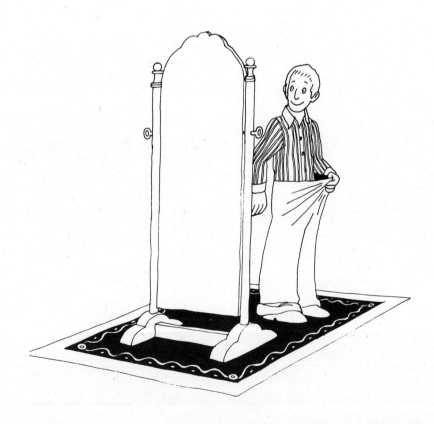

As can be seen from the preceding transcripts in this chapter, each of these people, Eric, Janet, and Albert put a great deal of energy into ignoring information, avoiding decision making, and refusing to deal with basic issues. In short, they were resistive to change, even though the desire was there. Though each was resistive, they did make new decisions and did make important positive changes. They discovered that while change is difficult, it is possible. Most of all, they discovered that they can be in control of their own lives.

V

HOW TO TRY HARD AND GET NOWHERE

As you have seen in previous chapters, people change their feelings, behaviors, and basic patterns of living by working through their problems in therapy. Many people, however, come for treatment in order to become more comfortable without making any *real* changes in themselves. Some of these people come with the idea that their problems will be magically solved by the therapist.

Others come into therapy just as an "excuse." Lucille is a good example. She had been in therapy for four years with another therapist and when her therapist moved out of town she came to see me. Lucille's problem, which she had already worked on for four years, was that her husband was upset because she would go to bed with almost any man she met. Her husband wanted her to be monogamous. Lucille did not want to be in a monogamous relationship, but she did want to remain married to her husband. She wanted to "have her cake and eat it, too," so to speak. So the way she had handled this problem with her husband was to say, "I am working on this in therapy but I can't find out why I do it." Her being in therapy was a way to satisfy her husband but in reality was an excuse to not have to change. After all, she *was* working on the problem. The game Lucille was playing was "Wooden Leg,"[23] or "what can you expect of a woman who is in therapy?" When I confronted Lucille about her behavior and her "Wooden Leg," "What do you expect of a woman in therapy? . . . certainly not to stay out of another man's bed," she left me for another therapist. She wasn't anywhere *near* ready to give up her excuse or her alibi for playing around.

Other people continue to play their games and refuse to change because their payoff from playing the games often seems greater than the payoff for changing. For example, take a man who has always felt and acted like a Victim in life. If he changes and starts to let people come through for him in a caring way, he must give up the image of a Victim. Then what will he have to talk or complain about? How will he get strokes? For most of us, there is a strong desire to change and grow, but there is also a pull to continue to live our lives as we have for so many years.

In the next section you will see people struggle hard to keep from changing and to hold on tightly to the old patterns of behavior.

In the first two transcripts you will see how two people threaten to leave the therapy group rather than change.

Dan wanted the group to support his being a Victim and when the group refused he threatened to leave. Dan's threat was intended to get the group to take care of him so that he didn't have to take responsibility for himself. In his life Dan often used the threat of leaving to avoid doing what he needed to do.

I'M GETTING OUT

DAN—I was in Chicago this weekend and I felt great! My time was structured; the people I was with really kept me on the go, and that's what I really need. If my time isn't filled up, I sit around and feel sorry for "poor old me." I know all this, but I don't seem to be willing to do much about planning my time myself. That's where I'm having trouble.

Doris—What do you want from the group, Dan?

DAN—When I came in here this morning, I wanted to make some contracts about structuring my time so I would feel better. Ever since JoAnn died, it's been so difficult for me to fill up my time.

Doris—Okay, what contracts do you want to make about filling up your time?

DAN—I don't know.

Doris—You do know! You know that structuring time is a way to help you feel good. You also know that when you don't plan things for yourself you start feeling depressed. You also know what you enjoy doing.

DAN—Well, then I really don't need to come to this group! [Said angrily.] That's *another* thought I had. I have the information *already* and maybe I should drop out of this group.

Doris—Okay.

DAN—Well, should I announce that I won't be coming back next week?

Doris—Should you?

DAN—Well, what I mean is, is this the way you do it?

Doris—Is that the procedure we use in this group?

DAN—Well, I guess it is. So next week will be my last week.

NICKY—You just decided right now to drop out of group?

DAN—Yes. . .well. . .No. . .but, if I have all the information. . .

Doris—Okay. I'm not going to play your game and I'm not going to rescue you.

DAN—What's my game? Doris, I'm so unaware of it, if it's a game.

Doris—What game did you just play, Dan?

DAN—Well, I kicked you by saying I was going to leave the group . . . "NIGYSOB" . . . If you won't tell me what to do, I'll leave.

Doris—That's right, Dan, you do know the game. I'm not willing to do your work for you, Dan. You can decide what kind of contracts you want to make to fill up your time. And I'm not going to be conned by your threat to leave the group. If you want to leave the group, okay. I think it's a destructive thing for you to do. But I'm not going to coddle you to stay.

DAN—See, last week Nicky said . . .

Doris—I want you to respond to what *I* said.

DAN—Well, I can appreciate that.

Doris—What did I say to you?

DAN—You said that you are not going to coddle me. Also I need to think up my own contracts. You said that you were not willing to take responsibility for me.

Doris—Right!

DAN—I wasn't aware that all of that was going on at all.

Doris—Okay, so now that you are aware, what are you going to do?

DAN—I am scared about coming to this group, Doris.

Doris—You didn't answer the question.

DAN—I feel like there is something to work on and I cannot get in touch with that something to work on.

Doris—You didn't answer the question.

DAN—I will come up with some contracts next week about how I can spend my free time.

Doris—Why?

DAN—Because I need to do it for myself to get out of this pattern of being depressed. I want to feel good about living. I'm also sorry about kicking you and the group.

As you can see, Dan had a big investment in not changing. This session was a turning point in Dan's therapy. The next week he came to group and made contracts to structure his time. Within several months he reported that he was feeling good. He was "too busy with all his activities" to be depressed, and he expressed his gratitude to the group for their not rescuing him several months ago.

In this transcript, Ann invoked a threat to leave her group because she was angry. Ann usually found someone to blame whenever she didn't come through for herself. She had been in group over a year and had threatened to leave at least once a month.

I'M GETTING OUT TOO!

ANN—I want to work. This week I tried to get ten positive strokes for myself and I didn't have time. Ten is a lot! [In response to some nonverbals in the group.] Ten is not a lot?

PAT—What was your contract?

ANN—I said I would get ten strokes for myself that would make me happy, and I came up with four. Maybe I did get more, but in my head I only came up with four and I feel good about that.

Doris—So how should we feel?

ANN—I think you should feel good that I came up with four. I feel happy.

Doris—Well, how should we feel, Ann, that you didn't keep your contract?

ANN—You could be angry. You could choose to be angry.

Elaine—You're smiling.

ANN—Yeah, because I don't think you should be angry. I really don't.

Doris—You set it up to kick people and you get kicked back. You know from past experience that if you come in and don't keep a contract we are going to confront you . . .

ANN—But . . .

Doris—Wait a minute. So you kick us by not keeping your contract and then we kick you back or you feel kicked because we confront you on not keeping your contract.

ANN—Doris, let me just say this. You came up with an arbitrary figure of ten. Where did you get off coming up with the figure of ten strokes?

Doris—You agreed to it, Ann.

ANN—I know, but I just . . .

Doris—It was your contract.

ANN—When you said ten strokes, I thought ten wouldn't be that hard; but ten strokes is a lot!

Doris—So it's "If It Weren't For You," Doris, I would have kept my contract.

ANN—No, I just think that ten strokes are too many to get.

Elaine—What could you have done when Doris suggested the number ten?

ANN—Well, I could have said, "Ten is too many, I want another number."

Elaine—That's right; so why didn't you?

ANN—Well, at the time I didn't think that . . . I didn't know that I wouldn't have time to get ten strokes.

Doris—I don't buy that. The contract you made was that you would get ten strokes for yourself. You said you needed more than one stroke per day. So what you did was not keep your contract and by doing that you kicked us; then we confronted you, which you perceived as a kick because you said, "After all, I got four strokes!" Then what you did was to kick us back by saying, "If it weren't for you, Doris, coming up with that arbitrary number; where do you get off coming up with ten?" So now we have the next move, which is for us to kick you, so within two minutes you have gotten to play out your favorite game, "Kick Me," twice; and you look as though you're ready for a third round. So let's stop. What do you want from the group, Ann?

ANN—Well, I just feel that maybe I need some other kind of therapy, because I don't feel like I'm getting anywhere in this group. It's too difficult. Maybe private sessions, or something—I don't know. Maybe I can't—I won't say can't—I won't go through this anymore. I would have tried to get more strokes, but this was a holiday weekend, and I knew that people had commitments, and I just didn't feel good about calling when they were probably with their families. I also have to work, and this is another thing —I simply don't have that much time to be in group.

Doris—Okay, what do you want, Ann?

ANN—I guess I'm going to get out of group because I'm just too frustrated. And my life is going by and I'm frustrated. I'm not going to go back to the way I was before I came here, because I've learned a lot since I've been in here; but apparently I'm not getting where *you* want me to be and . . .

Doris—Are you where you want to be?

ANN—Well, I don't want to be frustrated and terribly upset about this group and I have been.

Doris—You didn't answer the question. Are you where you want to be?

ANN—Well, I want to be happy.

Elaine—Where is that? You still haven't answered the question.

ANN—I don't know. I just don't know. Everything I do I just really feel that I'm not working the way I should be. I'm not where I want to be. I know I'm not. And also I just feel tired; very tired. Worrying from one week to another.

Elaine—What are we supposed to do?

ANN—Nothing. I don't expect anything from you. I think you have done a good job and I don't think it's your problem. I just feel tired.

Doris—That's a "Wooden Leg," Ann. What do you want?

ANN—I want to leave the group. So next week will be my last week.

Doris—Okay.

Because this time the therapists and the group had decided not to be uncomfortable with Ann's threat to leave the group, Ann was left with her threat. She did leave the group the following week. A month later, I received a call from one of Ann's friends saying how miserable Ann was and how terrible we were for kicking Ann out of the group. I responded by saying that if Ann wanted to come back, she could call. Ann did not call. She had successfully won at getting nowhere.

❖❖❖❖❖❖❖❖❖❖❖❖❖❖❖❖❖❖❖❖❖❖

The following transcript shows how Scott turned on scared feelings in order to avoid working in the group. His ultimate payoff was to leave the group without accomplishing anything.

When Scott was a child, he was told by his mother that he never did anything right. So Scott was living this out by never doing anything right. Paradoxically, Scott also was getting a lot of mileage out of being in group so that he could say, "What do you expect of a guy in therapy?"

ONE MESS UP AFTER ANOTHER

Scott—Well, I'm feeling scared.

Doris—Because?

Scott—I . . . I don't know . . . I don't know why. I'm feeling scared. I feel scared in here every week, and the closer the time comes to work, the more scared I get. You know, sometimes . . . I'm very relaxed until we sit down.

Doris—Okay. What are the different things you tell yourself in order to turn on the scared feelings?

Scott—[Pause] Let's see. "You gotta work . . ."

Doris—"You gotta work"—what else?

Scott—[Pause] I . . . I don't know! [Sounding exasperated] I just feel so sorry for myself.

Doris—You feel sorry for yourself. What does that mean? Mad, sad, glad, or scared?

Scott—Well, that's sad—no, scared.

Doris—You see what you do, Scott, is to choose to turn on certain feelings and the feeling you choose to turn on each time you come into the group is scared. You make that choice.

SCOTT—I see what you're saying. I . . . I want to fight that, though. I want to say, "I'm not really choosing that." I just fall into . . .

Doris—You don't just fall into feelings. You make a choice to feel a certain way. You also choose to escalate those feelings, or not to. So what would be an advantage of keeping yourself in a scared position in this group? What would happen?

SCOTT—I could ultimately leave the group because I can't do anything in here. I'll get the hell out of here.

Donna—Okay. How long are you giving yourself before you can justify saying, "If I don't get so far by such and such a time, I'm gonna leave."

Scott—Well, I've said that—I said—by the end of November one time.

Donna—Now when is it?

Scott—It's December. I've toyed with the idea of saying, "I want to leave; I want to get out." Uh . . . well, I'll quit after December is over.

Doris—Okay. So your payoff then is to keep yourself scared, not allow yourself to work, and then in the end you don't get anywhere and you can say, "I haven't gotten anything, so now it's okay to leave."

Scott—[Quietly] I suppose so.

Doris—It sounds to me like you're very heavily invested in not changing.

Scott—I would . . . I would agree with that.

Doris—So why are you wasting your time and money?

Scott—I come here—I can tell myself, "I really need help, I'm really in bad shape . . . poor Scott." And if I come to group therapy, that just emphasizes how bad off I am.

Doris—I see. Have you let anybody else know you're in group therapy?

Scott—A few people. Yeah. Not a lot of people, just close friends.

Doris—How about your close friends? Do they really think you're bad off 'cause you're in group therapy? Do you get any special treatment because people know you're in group? How about from your wife?

Scott—No, I don't think I get any special treatment.

Doris—You answered too quickly. I'd like for you to think about that.

Scott—Okay. Doris, that was a very interesting thing you said before that it looks like I'm heavily invested in not changing. I thought that was . . . that's true.

Doris—So maybe you want to think about leaving the group then.

Scott—I've been thinking about it since I started.

Doris—I think you need to make some kind of a decision and let us know next week. Either you decide to leave the group, or choose to stay in the group and come back with specific things you want to work on. If you decide to leave the group, you let us know next week, and then you have to come back one more week. That's how it works.

Scott—Okay.

Brenda—I don't want you to leave the group, Scott.

Lisa—Scott, don't leave the group, because only through the group can you help yourself.

Doris—Scott's gotten that information in here before, Lisa. Telling him, "This is the only place you can really make it," won't help. It's not going to change what he really wants to do. If Scott chooses not to make changes in his life, he could be in group therapy for five years and it won't make any difference. I'm much more aware now of people who are not willing to change, and I'm not willing to work with them, because in the end I feel angry. They haven't gotten anywhere, they've wasted a lot of money and a lot of their time and my time.

Scott returned the next week with the decision to leave group. He said that he understood what he needed to change, but he did not want to do anything about it.

❖❖❖❖❖❖❖❖❖❖❖❖❖❖❖❖❖❖❖❖❖❖

Another way people can get nowhere in therapy is to present a different problem to be worked on each week. It looks as though they are working hard, but rarely is anything accomplished. They make a contract and forget about it as soon as they leave group; or they remember from time to time during the week but do not follow through on the contract. Most often they do not even report back to the group about the contract. Each week the person is off and running about some new problem.

In this next transcript Joyce is a good example of someone who was following this pattern. Each week she looked as though she was working hard. She would get lots of information and make contracts. The following week Joyce would ignore the work from the previous week and bring up another issue to work on.

THE CASE OF THE MISSING CONTRACTS

JOYCE—I've got good news. I told Andy that I was going out of town next weekend and he said, "Fine, you're free to do what you want to do and that's okay with me." So I made my reservation and I feel really good.

LYNN—When do you go?

JOYCE—This weekend. I leave tomorrow at 6:50 P.M.

MARSHA—Who's Andy?

JOYCE—He's the guy I've been dating lately.

MARSHA—Is he the one from New York?

JOYCE—No . . . no . . . he's the one I met in California.

Doris—Wait a minute! Joyce, you have a contract from last week. You need to report on that first. You know you have been confronted on making contracts and not keeping them.

JOYCE—Oh yeah, I was to tell you what I was going to do about what I worked on, which was about being deserted and abandoned. And I decided that, um . . . that it boiled down to that I was afraid of being abandoned, and that's why I was afraid of telling Andy about my wanting to go away for the weekend, and I came up with something in relation to that and that was that when I was younger . . . um . . .

Doris—You're not making any sense. I want to stop you before we get into something else. What I want to find out specifically is what did you understand by the contract you made last week? I remember it quite differently.

JOYCE—Okay, I thought it was to . . . to just tell what I worked on and tell the group how I had acted and what I had done.

EILEEN—It wasn't that. It was something about . . .

Doris—I think Joyce needs to remember because she made the contract and this has happened several times. You make a contract, Joyce, and then when you come back the following week, you don't present the same contract that others remember; or you're unclear about the contract.

JOYCE—Okay.

Doris—It's your contract, so why don't you remember your contract?

JOYCE—I don't know.

Doris—Last week you got a lot of good information and you were supposed to be putting it together. You made a specific contract about that.

JOYCE—Okay.

Doris—So I'm not willing to work with you until you come up with what the contract was.

JOYCE—Okay.

Joyce repeated the same pattern during the next three sessions. Each time she was stopped and told that no one would work with her until she reported on the contract she had originally made. At the fourth session Joyce did report on her contract, which was her first step in breaking one of her patterns of trying hard and getting nowhere.

❖❖❖❖❖❖❖❖❖❖❖❖❖❖❖❖❖❖❖❖❖❖❖

Sandy was having an affair and her husband found out about it. Because she was afraid her husband would divorce her, she raced to therapy to placate him. I told her that her first task would be to make a decision—either work on your marriage and give up the affair, or get out of your marriage, or decide to stay in your marriage and tell your husband you were not going to end the affair nor did you want to end the marriage. If you made the latter decision, then you and your husband would need to decide if you still wanted to work on the marriage together. She made the commitment that she would come into therapy to work on making that decision. We agreed that she would make that decision in three months. I soon discovered that while Sandy was willing to work hard on other issues, she carefully avoided working on the major issue which had brought her into therapy.

PLAYING FAIR WITH AN AFFAIR

SANDY—I'd like to announce that last week I was asked to take over the position of Student Coordinator. This job would involve seeing that all the students have placements for their teacher training next year . . . and I turned the position down.

GROUP—Hurrahs and clapping.

JIM—That is really good, Sandy.

SANDY—Yes. I'm determined to stop playing the game of "Harried." There is always one more position, one more project, and I refuse to work myself to death.

LINDA—Great.

MAT—That's really good that you are taking care of yourself.

PENNY—I agree.

Doris—Are you hearing the strokes, Sandy?

SANDY—Um hmm . . .

Doris—Well, I noticed that Jerry didn't stroke you for turning down the position that you were offered. And immediately after you made the announcement, you looked at Jerry; so what is going on?

SANDY—Well, I was aware that Jerry didn't smile and didn't stroke me.

JERRY—I want to respond. I didn't feel good when I heard that Sandy didn't take the position at the university. I think people should work hard and go after the promotions, so even though it's good for Sandy that she is giving up her game of "Harried," I find it hard to be happy.

SANDY—Yeah . . . and I guess I was looking at Jerry for approval because I know that he too gets himself in the same rat race.

Doris—So you were getting lots of good strokes from the group and you gave the power to Jerry's Critical Parent and you didn't hear us.

SANDY—Um humm . . . Okay everybody, thanks for the support. My decision was and is a good one for me. One more thing I want to talk about. I've been thinking that I need to work on giving more strokes and getting more strokes from my husband.

Doris—Okay, Sandy. I'm unwilling to work with you on the issue of getting or giving more strokes to your husband, Paul. When you first came to see me three months ago you said that you were unhappily married, involved in an affair, and weren't sure what you wanted to do about your marriage. At that time I said you first needed to make a decision about what you wanted to do about your marriage.

SANDY—Right.

Doris—And the agreement was that you would make a decision in three months after evaluating all the facts. It's been over three months, so I want to know what is going on.

SANDY—Well, I haven't been able to make a decision yet.

Doris—You haven't worked on the problem; and I'm unwilling to work with you on anything else until this issue is resolved.

SANDY—Okay.

The Following Week

SANDY—I want to start tonight. I feel mad at you, Doris, because of last week. You said that I was giving all the power to Jerry and you didn't say specifically how I was doing that. So in the future, I want you to be more specific [said angrily]. Another thing, when you were working with Jerry and he didn't answer you right away, you started counting. I think that was really mean.

Doris—Let's deal with one issue at a time. First, I was very specific about how you were giving Jerry the power.

SANDY—I certainly don't remember.

Doris—Well, I did tell you that you were looking at Jerry when people were stroking you and you were discounting other people's strokes and giving all the stroking power to him.

SANDY—Oh yes, now I remember that.

Doris—About my counting. As you know, when Jerry is asked a question he takes a long time to answer. So I was calling the long pauses to his attention by counting.

ELENORE—Jerry was persecuting us by making us wait. He was persecuting you, too. And now you're rescuing him, Sandy, and persecuting us. I feel mad at you.

Judy—I think something else is going on, Sandy. Last week Doris confronted you about making a decision about your marriage and you said that you would think about it. So how were you feeling when she confronted you?

SANDY—I wasn't feeling mad.

Doris—Well, you've done some very angry things in here today. You blocked out the information I gave you last week. Then you rescued Jerry and persecuted the group and me. That's angry behavior.

SANDY—Well, I don't see it that way. I did make a decision about my marriage and that is, I'm going to stay in my marriage and continue to have an affair.

Doris—All right. That's your decision; however, I won't continue to see you in therapy unless your husband comes in and I make it clear to Paul in a session with the two of you that you are not seeing me in therapy in order for you to give up the affair.

SANDY—You've got to be kidding!

Doris—Nope. I'm not kidding.

SANDY—Okay. I'll need to think about whether I'm willing to do that.

Doris—Right, and let us know by next week.

In the next session Sandy said she had had a very hard week. For three days she had been furious with me and was going to leave the group. She said she had said over and over that I had no right to tell her that she had to bring her husband in and tell him of her decision not to end the affair. By the fourth day she had calmed down. Finally, she said she had felt relieved. She then said that she had reevaluated and had made the decision to end the affair and to work on the marriage. She had asked her husband to join her in marital counseling; she had never wanted that before. He agreed and I have now been seeing them together for the last four months.

❖❖❖❖❖❖❖❖❖❖❖❖❖❖❖❖❖❖❖❖❖❖❖

Rita was continually working hard in group (or so it appeared). She would come to the group with a specific problem to work on, get lots of strokes and feedback, and make a contract about what she could do differently. The next week she would report back as to how helpful the contract was, and then she would be off and running on another problem. Three months later, the same problem that she had originally worked on would again become an issue. After this happened several times, the pattern became clear. Rita was mainly working to please the group, and not working for her own growth and change.

IMPOSSIBLE!

RITA—I'd like to work. And I'd like to start out by saying that I feel angry at you, Janet, for taking so long to work tonight. I thought you did a lot of stalling around when you were asked a question. I'm also angry with you, Les, for the same thing.

STEL—I didn't see Janet stall at all . . . nor did I see Les do any stalling around.

Rita—Well, okay. That's what I saw.

Doris—The next time you feel angry about the way someone is working, I would like you to confront the person at that time.

Judy—I agree. Anger is a feeling that a person uses to motivate another person to change. If you confront Janet and Les now there is no way for them to change their behavior, and really no way to check out if they were stalling.

Rita—All right. Then I'd like to report on the contract I made last week. I made a contract to take the time to have at least one lunch date this week. I did that. In fact, I made *six* new friends. I went out to lunch twice, breakfast once, and the show once, and I played tennis twice. And all those dates were with different people. [Rita looks around and no one responds either verbally or nonverbally.]

Howard—Are you finished, Rita?

Rita—Yes.

Howard—Okay, I'll work.

Doris—Hold on. Something is going on. When someone makes a contract and then reports back that they have kept their contract, we usually stroke that person. So I'm wondering how people are feeling, because no one stroked Rita for keeping the contract.

George—Well, I'm feeling mad at you, Rita. First, I didn't like the way you said you were mad at Janet and Les. I thought you were kicking both of them. They both worked hard and got somewhere and I think you kicked, but it was hard to really tell.

Stel—I felt mad at you, Rita, when you talked about the stalling around. Also, I felt mad about your saying that you kept your contract, but I can't figure out exactly why. Like, I usually feel glad when people keep their contracts.

Doris—Say it as a six-year old, Stel.

Stel—Um . . . Yeah, I feel mad at you, Rita. You're such a show-off. Instead of one date, you had to go and make *six new friends in one week*. I don't believe it.

Doris—It was good the way you put your thinking and feeling together, and got in touch with why you were mad.

HOWARD—I felt mad, too. You are so competitive. First you criticize how other people work and then you brag about what you did. Six friendships—like it's not real! Nobody makes six friendships in one week.

JONI—I wasn't aware of feeling anything when you first asked, Doris, but I know that I usually block out feeling mad . . . Yeah . . . I am mad, Rita. It's like you're running around in a circle, trying to please us and be better than us.

JASON—I didn't like what happened either. Each time Rita makes a contract, she goes overboard.

Doris—Tell Rita.

JASON—You go overboard, Rita. And this happened in the past, but I don't think you really accomplish anything because two months later you will be back talking about having no friends again. So it's like you do the work in here for us, not for you. So . . . I also feel sad. Sad that you need to perform for this group instead of making changes for yourself.

HOWARD—That is really good feedback, Jason.

Doris—I felt mad, Rita, at the way you gave your feedback to Janet and Les. The timing made your feedback a kick to them. Also, I felt sad when you talked about making six new friends. A friendship takes time, and people don't make a friendship over one lunch or tennis game. I know you got a lot of negative feedback; but I think that what people said is important and I want you to think about it.

RITA—It's hard, but I'm hearing what people are saying.

Judy—I agree with Doris. The feedback is probably hard to hear, but you are in this group because you don't have many friends, so perhaps this will give you some information as to why people leave you or don't choose to get in a relationship with you.

RITA—Okay.

Judy—Doris, I think it was really neat the way you picked up on the covert stuff that was going on and asked everyone to say how they were thinking and feeling.

Doris—Thanks, Judy.

HOWARD—Yeah. I wanted to get on with it and not deal with my feelings with Rita because I was so mad. So by my not saying anything when Rita reported on her contract, I was covertly "getting" her.

Doris—You're right.

STEL—It's called being passive aggressive. We all got to get Rita with our passivity and look like the good guys.

JASON—What I like about this group is how smart we all are.

HOWARD—I'll second that.

The next week Rita reported that she could see why the group had been mad at her. It had been grandiose for her to say she had made six new friends. She also realized that this was a pattern of hers—she would figure out what she needed to do to please the group instead of solving her problem. The group and Rita became increasingly aware of this pattern in the sessions that followed. Rita still tries to please or "better" others; but she is doing it less because of the group's continual confrontations and their support and strokes when she solves problems for herself.

VI
THERAPISTS ARE HUMAN TOO!

The time has come to dispel the myth that therapists are godlike and can do no wrong. If you don't care to dispel the myth, well, then, just advance to Chapter VII. If you want to drop the notion that therapists belong to the realm of the heavenly instead of the human race, however, then read on. No doubt the myth has its origins both in the mind of a fellow traveler, who arrives with childlike hope for a magical cure, and the mind of the therapist, who naturally goes for the idea of being a god.

Therapists tend to perpetuate the notion that they are direct descendants of the Archangel Michael. Many seldom, if ever, admit to a mistake, nor do they allow, or in any way encourage confrontations by their fellow travelers. Furthermore, by being mute about their personal lives, they often appear to have no problems of their own.

Fellow travelers also tend to relish the myth that therapists aren't of the human race. They do not want to see a therapist who claims his/her humanness and even further, admits his/her mistakes or weaknesses. They want to see an all-knowing "Mother" or "Father" who will take care of them and solve all their problems.

The truth is that even though we often act like we think we are gods, and my fellow travelers desire such gods, we are not. Being human, we get angry, scared, and sad, and we don't always deal with these feelings in an appropriate manner. We make mistakes, and we too are in the process of growth and change.

In this first transcript, I am the therapist working with Nancy. She hadn't kept the contract which she had made with me and the group the previous week and I wasn't willing to make a new contract with her this week. Of course, I rationalized such a decision in the most theoretical terms. But the underlying truth was that I was mad because I had worked hard the week before to make a contract with Nancy, and now she was telling me that she had not kept her contract.

TO EXERCISE OR NOT TO EXERCISE . . .
OVER MY DEAD BODY

NANCY—I made a contract last week to do ten minutes of exercising every day and then to reward myself by watching television. I want to report that I didn't keep it [said in a flippant manner].

Doris—Because?

NANCY—Because I don't think the reward of watching television was strong enough. I found that I wasn't home very much this week. I had lots of things to do and I didn't get a chance to watch television and so . . . um . . . I'd like to re-negotiate the contract because I think the reward needs to be stronger.

Doris—What do you want for a reward?

NANCY—Uh . . . I think I would . . . uh . . . like to call somebody in the group to see somebody in the group after I have done my exercises and tell them that I've done them and have them give me a positive stroke, or say, "You did a really good job."

Doris—Well, that feels uncomfortable to me.

NANCY—Well, what I could do then, I guess, is think of some other reward I can give myself if I exercise.

Doris—Do you really want to make a contract about exercising?

NANCY—Yeah, I really do, but watching television as a reward is not strong enough. I put it off too easily because I have other things to do. Last week I was pretty uncomfortable about making the contract, but I thought that it would be a pretty good one because I like to watch television and I don't get to watch it very much.

Doris—Okay, um, well, I'm unwilling to work with you any longer because you didn't keep your contract. So why don't you decide what you want to do about exercising and how you will reward yourself, and tell us at the end of the group.

Carla—You didn't accept the contract that she made, Doris and I have some questions about that. I didn't see why the contract wasn't valid. Nancy said, "I want to make a contract to exercise every night and in order to reward myself, I'm going to call someone and get a stroke." So I'm having difficulty understanding why Nancy's contract wasn't valid. It seems to me that would have been okay.

Doris—Okay. The reason I didn't make the contract with Nancy was because she didn't come up with anything she could do to get strokes. Oh . . . except the contract, yeah . . to call people in the group. I saw that as setting us up as parents and then what would happen was . . . uh . . . we would say, "That's good, Nancy," and stroke her out of a Parent position and Nancy wouldn't develop her own Parent.

Carla—I saw it as Nancy saying, "I did a good thing, I exercised and I'm asking for reinforcement." I saw it as sort of the same thing as the contract we made with Tom. What would be the difference in Tom saying, "I cleaned my room and I want you to come and see it," and getting stroked for that and Nancy saying, "I did my exercises and, uh, I want to tell you about it" and then getting stroked for that?

Doris—Yeah, humm.

Carla—I thought it was a straight thing and I was confused about why you didn't make the contract.

Doris—Mainly because it felt right not to make the contract.

Carla—Yeah, you said that, and on the other hand, it felt right to me to make the contract and I couldn't understand why you didn't.

Doris—Um humm.

JOANNE—Can you explain about what makes a good contract?

Carla—I see that there's a split between Doris and me and what you did was ask a question that seems way off. I think you're rescuing and so I'm wondering how you're feeling.

JOANNE—Um . . . I was feeling angry.

Carla—Okay, would you say, "I'm feeling angry because . . . "

JOANNE—I'm feeling angry because I don't like people to disagree and I also feel scared because of the disagreement.

Doris—I understand. You feel scared because here are two people who are supposed to know what to do, and who are disagreeing.

TERRY—I feel glad because I think the disagreement is healthy. I think it reassures me that we don't all have to see things exactly the same way and I like that. I want to ask a question. [Looking at Doris] I don't understand how Joanne's statement was a Rescue.

Doris—Okay, you're asking me the question, Terry, and I'd prefer for Carla to answer because she called Joanne on the Rescue.

TERRY—Would you answer the question, Carla?

Carla—It's a Rescue because I was disagreeing with Doris, and what Joanne did was completely change the subject; which is a way of dissipating the tension in the group, rather than dealing with the real problem.

Doris—And the reason I had you ask Carla the question, Terry, was because Carla was the one who did the confronting. If I had answered you, then I would be discounting Carla. Carla and I are already disagreeing about Nancy's contract, so if I answer a question that should be directed to Carla, I would be playing "Two Against One" . . . you and me against Carla.

TERRY—Okay. I see that. I was on the triangle. I was Rescuing you and Persecuting Carla.

The Following Week

Doris—I want to start out tonight by talking about last week and why I didn't want to make the contract with Nancy. I said, "I felt uncomfortable . . . uh . . . I don't know exactly what it is, Nancy, but I don't want to make the contract with you." After the group, Carla and I were rehashing what went on, and I said, "I don't know why I didn't make that contract with Nancy, because when you ran it out, Carla, it sounded perfectly logical to me that I should have made that contract." I thought about it some more, and all of a sudden I knew what the uncomfortable feeling was. It was anger. I was angry with you, Nancy, because of the flippant way you said you didn't keep your contract when you first presented it. I felt angry, but what I didn't do was identify the feeling. So my anger was expressed by refusing to make a valid contract with you. I'm sorry that I was not in touch with my anger, and that I refused to make the contract.

NANCY—I'm glad you've explained what was going on, Doris. I was scared when you wouldn't make the contract. I couldn't figure out what was wrong; I was also mad. I was even more frustrated when Carla said she didn't understand why you didn't make the contract. I understand now. I think it takes a lot of courage for you to come in here and tell us—me—what you did. You could have dropped it. I accept your apology, Doris. I also want to say that I'm sorry I kicked you last week by flaunting the fact that I hadn't kept my contract.

Doris—Thanks. You're right, it's not easy to admit one's mistakes. But I do feel better now that I've straightened things out.

❖❖❖❖❖❖❖❖❖❖❖❖❖❖❖❖❖❖❖❖❖❖

In one therapy group we work for an hour, then take a ten minute break, and then work for another hour. At the beginning of the break time Jeff asked what appeared to be an "innocent question." I chose to answer his question, and Jeff and I were off and running around the triangle.

TIME OUT

JEFF—I would like some help in getting a glass of water. [Jeff is on crutches.]

Doris—I'll bring you a glass of water, Jeff.

JEFF—Thanks.

Carla—You just Rescued Jeff, Doris. Jeff didn't ask anyone to get him a glass of water. Jeff made a *grand* announcement to the whole group. "I'd like some help with a glass of water." The people in here who are Rescuers raced to the Rescue position on the triangle.

Doris—Like me. I agree; I did Rescue you, Jeff. You need to ask someone specifically for what you want.

JEFF—[Smiling] I would like a glass of water. Hank, would you get me a glass of water please?

Doris—Well, that's what happens to Rescuers, they soon turn into Victims.

After the Break When The Group Has Started Again

Doris—I want to make a couple of comments. At break time Jeff said he wanted some help in getting a glass of water, but he didn't ask anyone specifically. So, I came in for the Rescue. I was going to take care of Jeff. I also discounted the fact that Jeff could ask someone for what he wanted. Carla confronted the Rescue. Then I said, "Jeff, you need to ask someone specifically for what you want." At that moment, Jeff grinned, looked at Hank, and asked Hank to get him a glass of water. So I moved from the Rescue position to the Victim position on the triangle, and Jeff moved from the Victim position to the Persecutor position.

JEFF—I see. I put myself in the Victim position by not asking someone to get me a glass of water, and also I didn't have to take the chance that someone would say "no" to me.

Doris—Also, Jeff, you set it up so people could fight over who would get your water.

JEFF—I can see that. Then I Persecuted you, Doris, because you agreed with Carla that you had Rescued me. I didn't want to admit that I was being a Victim and asking for a Rescue.

GROUP—[Laughter] Who does!

HANK—I also got into a game. I Rescued you, Jeff, and I Persecuted you, Doris. At the time that Jeff asked me to get him the water I felt glad. Glad that he asked me instead of you, Doris, but at the same time, I didn't want to get up and get the damn water.

JEFF—Sounds like I needed to wind up with no water.

SHARON—You're back on the triangle acting like a Victim again Jeff and being a Persecutor to us.

JEFF—Okay. You're right and I don't need to be on the triangle.

❖❖❖❖❖❖❖❖❖❖❖❖❖❖❖❖❖❖❖❖❖❖❖

All people, including therapists, play games because games are a way to feel good about oneself on a temporary basis. Games also help people get positive and negative strokes, fill up time, and reaffirm early decisions about themselves and others.

The trouble with games is that along with the positive strokes there are always negative strokes. Games also block intimacy, and in the end make us and others not okay.

BIG GAME HUNTING

VIRGINIA—I have some unfinished business from the last group session. What's been going on with me all week is that I've been really angry a lot of the time.

Doris—Okay . . . uh . . . I was under the impression that last week we dealt with the issue of your being angry and you said you were resolved. Did you have a contract to continue with the issue of your anger this week?

TRUDY—Yes, she did.

Doris—Wait a minute, Trudy. I'm asking Virginia.

VIRGINIA—Yeah, I did. I think the contract I made was that I was to find out what was going on with me and report back to the group.

Doris—Okay, what did you figure out?

VIRGINIA—I was angry with Jill about the statement she had made to me in the group last week about my always being sick. I think it was a jab.

Carla—Hold on. I'm confused about the contract. I do know you had a contract to report back about what was going on with you last week in the group, but I thought this particular issue with you and Jill had been resolved. So I'd like clarification from other people.

GREG—My recollection was that the contract was for Virginia to deal with the anger she felt before she had gotten mad at Jill in the group.

Doris—Hmm . . . I don't remember it that way, Greg. Does anyone else remember what her contract was?

PATTY—I thought the contract had something to do with the way Virginia kept making comments in the group after the issue between her and Jill had supposedly been resolved.

PHIL—I thought you suggested to Virginia that she figure out why she kept interrupting the group last week and what advantages there were in doing that.

BARRY—I didn't hear it that way, but I'm not sure what the contract was.

Doris—Okay, what I'd like to do is drop the issue because everyone is remembering the issue differently.

PATTY—Yeah. At the end of the group last week Carla said, "I want you to think about what you're doing tonight and report on what's going on with you." That's what I thought happened.

Doris—So Virginia was to report on the advantages of interrupting the group?

PATTY—That's my recollection of what went on.

Carla—I think there's a game going on right now, but I'm not clear about what the game is.

Doris—I agree that there's some game going on. So suppose everyone states what they're feeling and thinking and maybe we can get to the bottom of this.

BARRY—Okay, I'm feeling mad because of the fog and confusion.

Doris—I'm feeling scared because I don't know what the hell's going on. I'm also angry with you, Virginia, because you are unclear.

PATTY—I feel scared because things are mixed-up and damn mad because we're wasting time and Virginia is the center of attention once again.

JILL—I'm feeling angry because things are so confused.

LOU—I'm feeling angry because I think I did understand what was going on.

MARILYN—I'm feeling angry also because we seem to be getting into another mess with Virginia as the center of attention.

TRUDY—I feel angry because things aren't resolved.

GREG—[Said in an angry tone] I'm angry because I thought Virginia was clear and it was the other people in the group who got things confused.

Doris—Okay, who do you see as the responsible person, Greg?

GREG—I guess I think that you are, Doris. Last week Carla made a suggestion for Virginia to think about things and she was reporting on that when she came in tonight.

Doris—So you think I'm responsible for the mess.

VIRGINIA—I'm angry at you too, Doris, because it was clear to me what I was supposed to do, and I'm angry because of the group's response to me.

CAROLINE—I'm scared because I don't know what's going on and I don't remember the contract, and I'm mad because we're not getting anywhere.

Carla—Okay, I'm scared and mad. Scared because I don't know what's going on and mad because things are once again confused with Virginia in the center. I think you've kicked the group, Virginia, because you're acting as though it is our problem that we didn't understand the contract, when in fact you weren't clear about it yourself. First you said you *thought* the contract was such and such, and now you're saying you *know*. So you pulled a switch.

VIRGINIA—I don't think I switched.

Doris—Baloney! You weren't certain about your contract nor were other people in this group. That's where the confusion began. Then what happened is that we all took sides.

CAROLINE—Uproar!! That's the game! Uproar.[24]

Carla—You're right, it is "Uproar."

Later The Same Evening . . . More Games

Doris—Who wants to work?

VIRGINIA—I do. I want to ask each person in the group for a stroke. I know this will make me feel better.

Doris—Okay.

VIRGINIA—Patty, would you tell me something that you like about me?

PATTY—Okay, I like the way you're wearing your hair tonight.

VIRGINIA—Thank you. Caroline, I'd like you to tell me something *you* like about me.

CAROLINE—I won't tell you something I like about you because I'm still feeling mad at you.

VIRGINIA—Jill, I'd like a hug from you.

JILL—I don't want to give you a hug right now. I think there's something going on, but I don't know what it is.

VIRGINIA—Carla, will you give me a hug?

Carla—I don't want to give you a hug, Virginia. I'm feeling scared about what you're asking for. I think you're setting yourself up to be kicked by people in this group. After all that's happened, and how mad people have been, do you really feel safe asking people in here for what you want?

VIRGINIA—No.

Carla—Okay. I suggest that you ask people how they're feeling toward you before you ask them for what you want.

Doris—I see it differently. I think a good way to get out of feeling bad is to ask for strokes. Some people do have residual anger from what happened earlier and can choose not to stroke Virginia. If they tell her they don't want to stroke her, she doesn't have to be a Victim. On the other hand, some of the people in here will stroke her. So I'd like you to continue with the exercise, Virginia.

VIRGINIA—Right. Okay, I'd like a hug, Trudy.

TRUDY—Okay.

VIRGINIA—Thank you. Doris, I'd like a hug.

Doris—I'd like to give you a hug.

VIRGINIA—Lou, I'd like you to tell me something you like about me.

LOU—Okay, I like your enthusiasm for things; also, your warmth.

VIRGINIA—Marilyn, I'd like for you to tell me something nice.

MARILYN—Sure. I like your intelligence and I also think you have a pretty face.

VIRGINIA—Barry, I'd like a hug from you.

BARRY—Okay. I also like the way you kept asking for good stuff and didn't get scared when you didn't get what you asked for.

PATTY—I think you did a lot of hard work tonight, Virginia. I think it's good that you asked for strokes in the group.

CAROLINE—Virginia, I refused to give you a stroke when you asked and I want to tell you the reason. The reason is because I'm *mad* at you. I think you take up lots of time in here and get lots of attention in unstraight ways. I didn't want to give you attention for that.

Doris—Okay, it's time to stop group. See you next week.

The Following Week—Clarifying the Games

Doris—Carla and I want to talk about what we saw happen last week. First of all, I want to start out with what we could have done to prevent the game of "Uproar" last week and how we all got into the game. When Virginia first presented what she wanted to work on, Carla or I or someone in the group could have stated that Virginia was not being clear about her contract. Instead of making an issue out of *what* the contract was, it would have been better to ask Virginia to list the advantages of being unclear. Or, we could have left her to think about the contract, and later she could have come back into the group when she had things clear. This would have put the responsibility on her. Okay, from what we can gather, here's how we got into the game. The con for the game was Virginia's unclearness, but it was Carla, and then I, who threw it open to the group by asking how other people remembered the contract. So this set up competition between people in the group as to who could remember the best, and consequently everyone was remembering something different. People got mad at each other and took sides. Thus, the game "Let You and Him Fight" was played out. As feelings escalated we were into "Uproar." Later in the evening, when Virginia was working for the second time, I was seated on the sofa opposite Carla, and I observed Carla and Caroline whispering to each other. I felt angry about that, particularly at Carla. What I said in my head was, "Carla should know better. She knows about group process and splitting groups and taking sides, and that's exactly what she's doing." What I didn't do was confront Carla and deal with my anger. Then later, when Carla told Virginia that she really felt uncomfortable about what she was doing and how she might be setting herself up for kicks by asking people who were probably still mad at her for good strokes, I discounted what Carla said, because I was mad at her. So I "got" Carla by disagreeing with what she was saying and then encouraged Virginia to go on. I also discounted other people because other people *were* feeling angry at Virginia. My justification was, "I feel okay about Virginia, why don't you?" (*My* feelings are *more* important than Carla's and the group's.) When I said, "*I* think we should go on," the power was split at that point, and the rest of the people in group stroked Virginia and took my side. My guess is that some people in this room discounted their anger at Virginia, went ahead and stroked her, kicked Carla by stroking Virginia, and stroked me by taking my side. Any questions so far?

GROUP—No . . . No . . . No.

Doris—Now, not only were Carla and I involved in the games last week, but also other people were involved. And so, we would like each of you to take responsibility for your part in the games.

The rest of the group members took responsibility for their part in the games and also stroked us for figuring out what had gone on the previous week. We were also stroked for being good models.

❖❖❖❖❖❖❖❖❖❖❖❖❖❖❖❖❖❖❖❖❖

Knowing that therapists are human may be scary, but our being human also allows for much fun, too.

One fall day the training group assembled. (In these groups people learn to be therapists by doing therapy with each other.) For me it was a very special day—my birthday. However, I had not shared this information with the group. I thought Carla was the only person who knew.

SURPRISE

Doris—Okay, who wants to be therapist today?

BECKY—I'll be therapist. Who wants to work?

WALT—I will.

BECKY—[Therapist] Okay, Walt. What do you want to work on?

WALT—I want to work on two things really. One thing is that I need to ask for what I want more often, and the other is, well, specifically, my birthday is coming up soon, and birthdays have always been like special, but not special.

BECKY—[Therapist] What does that mean, special but not special?

WALT—They've been special for me—inside; but like nobody else knows they're special. If I tell people that it's my birthday, and they say, "Happy Birthday," well it's nice but I don't really think they care because I have to remind them. If I don't remind them that it's my birthday I don't get any "Happy Birthday" said to me, and then I feel bad. What happens in my head is that I believe that the only strokes that are really powerful, the only strokes that are any good, are the ones I get from people who don't need to be reminded that it's my birthday. If somebody comes up to me and says, "Hey, Happy Birthday," I think "Wow, they *remembered*" and then I feel really good. But how they remember when I haven't told them in the first place? Yet, I was taught not to tell people about my birthday because it wasn't nice. I don't like being in this position.

BECKY—[Therapist] Okay, I see that as a really crucial issue for you, Walt, especially with all the feelings associated with birthdays, and what that means in this culture. That makes sense to me. What I see you doing is putting yourself in a corner. On the one hand you want to get what you want, but you want people to just *know* without your telling them. You want them to have a good time with you and let you know that they care about you. On the other hand, it's difficult because you think you should act proper and not say anything and take a chance on getting nothing. What I'd like for you to do is role play the part of you that wants to get what you want on your birthday by telling people and the other part that is afraid to tell people what you want because it isn't proper. Would you be willing to do that?

WALT—Okay.

BECKY—[Therapist] Okay. Why don't you be the part of you that's afraid to tell people that it's your birthday. And in the other chair you can role play the part of you that wants to tell people that it's your birthday.

WALT—Okay. You know, Walt, like it's so much better when somebody comes up to you and says, "Happy Birthday, Walt" and you haven't talked about it and it's just a surprise. They know it's your birthday and it just seems so much better.

[Walt switches chairs.]

Yeah, but if you want people to say "Happy Birthday" you need to ask for that. You need to let people know. That's the way you get it. People tell you good things and you feel good. You ask people and tell them to tell you.

[Walt switches chairs again.]

Yeah, that's some of it, but it isn't as good as if you're really surprised. It's like having a surprise party that you already know about.

BECKY—[Therapist] Is that the way it is Walt . . .the two parts of you?

WALT—Yeah.

BECKY—[Therapist] All right. I see you as not getting very far with that, so what I'd like is for you to use an alter ego and I want to know if there's anyone in the room who's in touch with this problem who would be willing to be Walt's alter ego.

[Group silence.]

SUSY—I don't understand what you're asking for.

BECKY—[Therapist] I want another person who would be willing to be the part of Walt that needs to get in touch with the part of him that wants to be taken care of. [Silence] What I was thinking, Doris, is that you could be the alter ego since it's your birthday!

[Group laughter, then the group begins to sing.]

GROUP—Happy Birthday to you, Happy Birthday to you . . .

Doris—[Loudly] Oh my goodness !!!

GROUP—[More laughter.]

Doris—I've never been so surprised. [Laughter] My gosh, thank you! [Laughter]

GROUP—You mean you didn't know?

Doris—I didn't know. I kept thinking what a coincidence! It's my birthday today and here is Walt having a birthday; I

wonder when his is. I thought you were doing a beautiful job with the therapy, Becky.

GROUP—[Laughter.]

Doris—Thanks everybody!

BECKY—You'd better say that, Doris. Walt and I rehearsed five times this morning.

VII
SELECTING YOUR MEDICINE MAN OR WOMAN

If you should ever decide to join a therapy group, the first thing you should do is to find a therapist who has been trained to lead groups.

Today groups are run by people in many different professions—social workers, psychologists, psychiatrists, ministers, nurses, and counselors. Who may lead a therapy group is often determined by the laws of the state in which one lives. Some states license therapists while other states have no licensing laws. Licensing, however, is not a good indicator of a therapist's ability or proficiency; nor is one's particular educational background. The best resource for finding a good therapist is often a friend who has been in therapy and has found it helpful.

Most group therapists will first see you at least twice on an individual basis before recommending that you enter a group. Once you have started a group, you may or may not continue individual sessions along with the group therapy sessions. This would depend on your particular needs.

Two months of therapy should be enough to help you evaluate your therapist and what you are getting out of therapy. Frequently, people are afraid to question their therapist and/or their therapy. They discount themselves by saying, "How do *I* know if my therapist is good? What right do *I* have to question? *After all*, the therapist is a professional and I don't know about such things."

I contend that you do know—especially after two months' time. You would be doing yourself a disservice if you did not ask yourself such questions as: Am I solving the problems that I wanted to solve? What changes have I made in my life since beginning group therapy two months ago? What *specific* changes can I list? How do I feel about these changes (if any)? Have they improved my life? If I can see no changes, that in itself may be a problem to be worked on. Am I really working to solve problems? Are other people in the group solving their problems? What changes have I seen take place in other people? Again, can I be specific and list these changes?

Does my therapist provide enough information about problem solving? Can I honestly confront my therapist with these questions? What do I expect from my therapist and the group therapy sessions?

After evaluating these questions, ask yourself, "What do I honestly think and feel about my therapy and my therapist?"

The reason that it is important to ask these questions is that very often people get involved and enmeshed in nonproductive therapy. Some groups merely stroke and indulge a person's problems, and some groups just talk about a person's problems. I also know there are groups that help a person solve problems.

I have a personal bias in what I think is good group therapy, as you may have noticed, and I invest a good deal of my time training and supervising therapists in the community. Training therapists is hard work because we therapists tend to be well-defended against bearing criticism; however, it is also very stimulating and rewarding to work with my colleagues. For me it has been an invaluable learning experience and I know that I have grown a great deal. I have decided to share with you portions of two actual training sessions, one, a transcript with beginning therapists and the other a training session for advanced therapists.

The first transcript is of the beginning therapists. The therapy students in the group have been together for five months. The group is structured so that each of the students takes a role of therapist or of fellow traveler in the group.

When a therapy student acts as the fellow traveler, s(he) works on actual problems in his/her life. These problems might be problems that the student is having in the classroom or problems that s(he) is having with his/her parents, spouse, or own children. This particular structure encourages students to look at themselves so they can become aware of their own weaknesses and strengths. It always amazes me that therapy students often deny that they themselves have problems. However, once they are given permission to admit they have problems, they are never at a loss as to what they can work on in a training session.

One of the reasons I have chosen this structure for the training and supervising of therapists is that this was one aspect of my own training and I know how valuable it was for me. We therapists learn how easily a therapist can confuse his/her own issues with the issues of the fellow traveler being worked with. Learning to separate one's own problems from fellow travelers' problems is a major step in becoming a good therapist.

In the role of therapist the student does therapy with a fellow student. If s(he) gets stuck, s(he) can stop the therapy, consult with me and then continue working, or s(he) can choose to stop working. I, too, have the option to stop the therapy and consult with the student therapist. At this point I may or may not work with the fellow traveler. After therapy has stopped, I give feedback to the student therapist and then both the student and our fellow travelers give feedback to each other, as is shown in the first transcript.

In training sessions with beginning therapists I model being a therapist first. I do this to show my students different things they might look for with their fellow travelers and different ways they might deal with problems when they themselves are the therapist. There are many things I teach students to think about. I encourage them to be aware of who is working harder —therapist or fellow traveler. If a therapist cares *more* about the person solving the problem than the person cares, the problem won't get solved . . . and the therapist will be frustrated. I also encourage students to recognize and stroke productive changes that their fellow travelers make. If a therapist holds back strokes and doesn't recognize when a fellow traveler has changed, the fellow traveler will most likely slip back to the old destructive behavior in order to get attention.

A TRAINING SESSION FOR
BEGINNING THERAPISTS

Doris—Today we are going to concentrate on contracts. First, we'll review what a contract is, why contracts are important, and what makes up a good contract. After that I will be the therapist and model making a contract with somebody. Then we'll rotate and each of you will be therapist and work with somebody who wants to make a contract. Since we've talked about contracts before, I would like for someone to volunteer to tell the rest of us what a contract is.

TAD—I'll do that, Doris.

Doris—Good, Tad.

TAD—A contract is an agreement that's made between the fellow traveler and the therapist for the fellow traveler to accomplish a clearly stated goal.

Doris—Good. Now in order for a contract to be valid what are the requirements?

MEL—I just studied that. The four basic requirements that must be met are that there must be mutual consent; that is, the therapist and his fellow traveler must be in agreement as to the goals. There must be valid consideration. That means that there is an exchange of goods. I give you an hour of therapy, you give me a bushel of corn.

GROUP—[Laughter.]

MEL—Another requirement is legal object. That means the contract must be legal and ethical.

SHELLY—You mean you wouldn't train a bank robber to be a better bank robber?

Mel—[Laughter.] Right. And the fourth requirement is competency. That means that we, the therapists, are adequately trained to do what we say we can do. Also, our fellow travelers must be competent to enter into a treatment contract.

Doris—Your answer is excellent, Mel.

Tad—Right on.

Doris—Now, how about an example of a treatment contract?

Tad—Hmm . . . Well, Shelly could make a contract to stop smoking or Bill could make a contract to intervene five times in the group each session in order to learn how to be active.

Doris—Fine . . . Now, before a therapist would make the contract with Shelly for her to give up smoking, what would the therapist need to check out?·

Shelly—The therapist would need to check out what the advantages are for me in giving up smoking. And, because I don't smoke, there wouldn't be any advantages. [Laughter]

Tad—[Laughter] Shelly, I won't make the contract with you since you don't need it.

Carla—[Laughter] Such a bunch of comedians!!

Doris—[Laughter] I agree. One more question. Why would a therapist even bother to make a contract with a fellow traveler?

Alex—I think it's important because the fellow traveler has to state specifically what he needs to do differently in order to change, and then he and the group have a way to check out whether or not he is doing what he said he would do.

Doris—Okay, but why does the group get in on the contract?

Bill—I think it's because the fellow traveler needs support and encouragement from the group, as well as the fact that he has to learn to deal with others if he doesn't keep his contract.

Doris—If the fellow traveler is interested in changing, why does he need the encouragement from the group?

BILL—Because changing behavior is hard and people need encouragement to change.

SHELLY—After a time the person has learned the behavior and is comfortable with it. The person has also internalized the encouragement and does it for himself.

Carla—That's neat. You really know your material on contracts.

Doris—I like the way people are getting the material down in here. Now let's put it to practice. I'll be the therapist and model making a contract with somebody and then we'll rotate. Who wants to make a contract?

MEL—I want to make a contract, Doris, around working on my voice, projecting my voice, if that's possible to do. I've gotten two evaluations back recently from two of my professors who have watched me do therapy and one of the main criticisms is that I have a low voice, that people have trouble hearing me, and I'd like to try and change it; but I'm not quite sure how to go about making the change.

Doris—Well, you said that you want to *work around* and you'd like to *try*, so I'm wondering what advantages there are in speaking in a low voice, Mel.

MEL—Um . . . people can't hear what I have to say. And if they can't quite hear, they are less likely to question me. Umm . . . I never thought about that.

Doris—Any other advantages?

MEL—People have to strain and they sit up and listen to me. I'm definitely in control of the situation.

Doris—Big advantages. So why would you want to give up those advantages?

MEL—Well, if people can't hear me, they eventually stop listening, so in the end I'm the loser.

Doris—Are there any other advantages of talking louder?

MEL—I would get more good strokes if people could hear what I say. People wouldn't get mad at me for talking low. The evaluations from my professors would be better.

Doris—Okay, it looks as though you are in touch with a number of advantages of talking louder, so what is the contract you want to make?

MEL—To talk with force . . . to talk loud . . . maybe even to exaggerate.

Doris—Great! Okay, how about making a contract in this group that you will magnify everything you say for two weeks, starting today.

MEL—Sounds good to me. I've always enjoyed being a ham. In addition, I'll probably get stroked immediately from the group because everyone will be aware that I am fulfilling my contract.

TAD—You're right!

MEL—Also I'll be pleasing my Parent, which says that I should be talking up because it's important that people hear me. And my Adult says that people who talk loud sound confident.

Doris—Right on. What's your contract, Mel?

MEL—I will magnify everything I say for the next two weeks. I'm finished working, Doris, I got what I wanted.

LOUIS—Fine work, Mel. And I see that you are already doing it.

BILL—I agree. That was a good contract you made for yourself.

Doris—Now who else would like to work as a therapist?

SHELLY—I'd like to be therapist.

Doris—Fine.

SHELLY—Who would like to make a contract?

ALEX—I'd like to make a contract to jog every morning for ten minutes.

SHELLY—[Therapist] Why do you want to jog?

ALEX—When I jog in the morning, I feel better for the entire day. It stimulates me. I function better. But what I don't like is giving up those extra ten minutes of sleep. I tend to get up at the last minute and then I have to hurry, miss breakfast and race to work; but if I take time to jog in the morning, I limber up and feel better.

SHELLY—[Therapist] Okay, I'd like to suggest that you do your jogging, but do it at a different time of day. That way you wouldn't have a problem.

ALEX—I don't mind jogging later in the day, but I also want to do it in the morning.

SHELLY—[Therapist] I won't accept that contract because, um . . it sounds to me like you'really going to have to push yourself and there's not that much in it for you.

Doris—Okay, let's stop, Shelly.

SHELLY—Okay.

Doris—What are you feeling right now?

SHELLY—I feel the same way I did when I started. I was scared. I've never done therapy before.

Doris—I understand that, but let's work with what is going on with you as therapist. What were you feeling when Alex said, "I want to get up in the morning and jog?"

SHELLY—I don't know about other feelings, but I was thinking that I know all about getting up early in the morning and I think Alex is really being hard on himself.

Doris—Is getting up in the morning a hassle for you?

SHELLY—Yeah. Getting up even ten minutes earlier would be a hassle for me.

Doris—Okay. So telling Alex, "Don't push yourself" was your issue and not his.

SHELLY—Umm . . . yeah. . . So then when I told Alex, "Do it in the afternoon when you're awake," I was doing it for me [Laughter].

Doris—Right. Okay, I'd like to give you feedback on your therapy. I'm glad you jumped in and got your feet wet, Shelly. The first time as a therapist in here takes lots of courage. Your voice was strong. You acted confident. And you didn't get defensive when I checked out if getting up in the morning was tough for you. You got in touch with how you were putting your own stuff on someone else and then laughed at yourself. Good job.

SHELLY—It wasn't as hard as I thought.

Doris—Would you tell us what you liked about your therapy?

SHELLY—What I liked was that I decided to be a therapist in the group and I *did* it.

Doris—Fine. Now would you give Alex feedback following the structure, "The time I felt closest and the time I felt farthest away."

SHELLY—Umm . . . The time I felt closest, Alex, is when you said you wanted to work with me. Also when you told me about how good jogging made you feel. The time I felt farthest away was when you talked about getting up early in the morning.

Doris—Fine. Alex, will you follow the same structure?

ALEX—Yeah. The time I felt closest, Shelly, was when you asked me why I wanted to jog. I thought you really cared and wanted to know. The time I felt the farthest away was when you suggested I jog in the afternoon.

Doris—Any further questions?

ANTON—Yeah. Why do you ask people to say when they felt closest and when they felt farthest away?

Doris—I think it is useful for people to get in touch with the fact that they *know* when they feel close and when they feel far away from other people. If the therapists starts to feel far away, he or she can use this information as a clue to what is going on in therapy. In addition, it is a way to get more information about yourself. Remember, Shelly has a hard time getting up in the morning and she felt farthest away from Alex when he talked about getting up early. Alex felt farthest away when Shelly was not picking up on what he wanted but instead throwing out what she wanted. Any more questions?

GROUP—No . . . No . . . No.

Doris—Who wants to be therapist next?

ALVIN—I do. Who would like to make a contract?

DEBBY—I would like to make a contract to always end my therapy hour with a fellow traveler on time. I tend to run over. Often, I should be ending at ten, but don't end until 10:20 or 10:30.

ALVIN—[Therapist] Why do you let your therapy hour go over?

DEBBY—Often I don't have anyone coming in for the next hour, so I don't have to pace myself. I don't have to watch the clock.

ALVIN—[Therapist] Can you think of any advantages for your fellow travelers if you end on time?

DEBBY—Well, I think that the biggest advantage is that I am offering them a model for their learning about being on time, and being organized. I think it's advantageous for them to have control in their life.

ALVIN—[Therapist] And what would be the advantages for you, Debby, if you stop your appointments on time?

DEBBY—Well, I can use the next hour more productively.

ALVIN—[Therapist] Are you in touch with any other reasons why you would let the hour go over, other than the fact that you don't have something scheduled for the next hour?

DEBBY—Yeah. I enjoy my work.

ALVIN—[Therapist] Is there any Rescuing, uh . . . I'm wondering if you are Rescuing your fellow travelers.

DEBBY—No! When I'm ready to wrap up an hour, I can with no problems.

ALVIN—[Therapist] Do you think the advantages you and your fellow travelers would gain if you ended on time are worthwhile advantages and enough reason for you to stop on time?

DEBBY—Yeah.

ALVIN—[Therapist] Okay. So suppose you make a contract with this group to stop each session on time for the next two weeks.

DEBBY—The only thing is that I'm kind of wondering what's my Child ego state going to get out of ending on time . . . *always* ending on time. I'm wondering what's my Child going to get out of all that paperwork.

ALVIN—[Therapist] I don't understand; what paperwork? What is that?

DEBBY—Well, you know, there's always a mountain of things to be read, journals I've never gotten into.

ALVIN—[Therapist] Now I get the picture. If you end your therapy session on time then you think you have to use the next hour for reading journals and doing paperwork. It sounds to me like what you really want is permission not to have to read so much and not to have to do the amount of paperwork that you force yourself to do.

DEBBY—I hear what you're saying. Maybe I need permission to stop reading so much. But then one side of me says, "It's true, I'm tired of reading all that stuff." But the other side says, "No, I really want to read the stuff." It's like I'm sitting on the fence.

ALVIN—[Therapist] What will you get out of it if you stop your appointments on time?

DEBBY—Not very much.

ALVIN—[Directed at Doris] Okay, I'm not sure at this time if I should be working with Debby on her giving herself permission to stop the paperwork, or if she should be working on stopping her appointments on time.

Doris—Alvin, let's stop. Debby, do you want to continue working?

DEBBY—Yeah. I think I'm on the right track.

Doris—What you said was, "It's like I'm sitting on the fence." So what alternatives do you see for yourself?

DEBBY—It's not that I'm doing so much reading, Doris. And I do need to study these journals to keep up.

Doris—You didn't answer my question.

DEBBY—When I'm not reading, I would like to be reading. But when it's time to read, I don't want to.

Doris—I'd like to give you some information. When you worked with Alvin, you started out working on closing your appointments on time. Just as he was about to make a contract with you, you switched. Then you started working on the issue of your paperwork and reading. But when Alvin suggested that you might want permission not to do so much reading and paperwork, you said you were on the fence. That's when I started to work with you, Debby. I asked you a question and you didn't respond. Then I asked again, and again you didn't respond. So I think you must be getting something out of stalling and switching. Think about it. Then come back in when you figure out what advantages there are in your stalling first with Alvin, then me, and also what you want for yourself.

DEBBY—Okay. I'll do that and come back in before end of group today.

Doris—Good. Okay, Alvin, I want to give you feedback about your therapy. In the beginning, I thought you asked two excellent questions, "What are the advantages to your fellow travelers in ending your session on time?" and, "What are the advantages for yourself?" The next thing you asked was, "Is there any Rescuing?" Did you think that Debby was Rescuing, Alvin?

ALVIN—[Laughter] Yes, I did.

Doris—Okay. So then it would be good to say, "Sounds to me like you're Rescuing your fellow travelers." I think your observation was good, and it might be an accurate one; but if you say to Debby, "Is there any Rescuing?" and Debby says, "No, I don't Rescue," you've gotten yourself into a corner.

ALVIN—So if I've got information, it's better for me to make a statement instead of asking a question.

Doris—Yes. Many times a therapist will ask a question when he already knows the answer. Then the fellow traveler doesn't confirm what he is thinking, or answer the way he wanted and he feels cornered. The reality is that the therapist puts himself in the corner. If he then states, "Well, I think you are Rescuing," the fellow traveler will most likely feel mad because the therapist has pulled a switch. After Debby said that she wasn't Rescuing, you moved into your Parent and suggested a contract which she at first accepted and then quickly rejected. I think at this point the two of you were in a power struggle. You were in your Parent trying to get her to do something and she was in her Rebellious Child.

ALVIN—Yeah, I was angry after she said she wasn't Rescuing. Then I got involved with permission. I kept thinking, "I'm off the track." And that would have been a good place to end it right there.

Doris—Right. It's okay to stop working with someone. If you think you aren't getting anywhere, give yourself permission to stop. It's better for you and your fellow travelers. You don't need to get into a power struggle. If your fellow traveler wants to work and solve the problem, he or she will be back working on the same issue until it gets resolved. Okay. Would you tell us what you liked about your therapy?

ALVIN—Um hmm . . . The thing I liked was the way I connected up Debby's appointments running over and her doing her paperwork.

Doris—Good. All right. Will you both give feedback about when you felt closest and when you felt farthest away?

ALVIN—Yeah. I felt closest to you, Debby, when I told you that I thought you needed permission to not have to do so much reading. I felt farthest away when you told me you weren't Rescuing.

DEBBY—I felt closest to you, Alvin, when you asked what advantages there might be for my fellow travelers if I stopped the appointment on time. And I felt farthest away when you stopped working with me and checked out with Doris what you should be working on.

Doris—Okay. Who would like to be therapist?

KATE—I'd like to be therapist.

BRIAN—And I'll work. I would like to make a contract to stop smoking. Last summer I gave it up, but then about four months ago, I started again.

KATE—[Therapist] Okay. What are the advantages of giving up smoking?

BRIAN—It will make me healthier. It will be better for my heart. My chances of surviving longer are better. What I know is that when I wasn't smoking, I felt a whole lot better. I had more energy . . . more money. I felt exhilarated.

KATE—[Therapist] All right. One thing I want to check out. Smoking is a form of self-stroking. For every smoke you have, you give yourself a stroke. How much do you smoke each day?

BRIAN—Well, let's see, about a pack and a half?

KATE—[Therapist] So that's thirty strokes you're giving up each day. One smoke equals at least one stroke. So what are you going to replace those cigarette strokes with?

BRIAN—Umm . . . Well, I can get strokes in here for not smoking.

KATE—[Therapist] Right. What other strokes will you get?

BRIAN—My family will be happy. They'll be happy that I stopped smoking. I can't think of any other strokes I'll get.

KATE—[Therapist] Well, why not buy yourself some new clothes? That would be a good way to stroke yourself.

BRIAN—I could do that.

KATE—[Therapist] Okay. So how about stopping smoking tomorrow morning?

BRIAN—Okay. Fine.

KATE—[Therapist] All right. I'll check with you in two weeks. Okay, I'm finished.

Doris—Kate, I liked the way you checked out the advantages for Brian in giving up smoking. Also, it was good the way you tied up smoking and stroking. Then what happened was that Brian got stuck and couldn't think of any ways to give himself strokes. You gave him an answer, "Try shopping."

KATE—[Laughter] Shopping works great for me!

Doris—[Laughter] Okay. It may also be a good stroke for Brian, but then again, it may not. That's why I think it's better to let the person figure out the strokes they like best.

BRIAN—Yeah. I should have mentioned to Kate that I'm sort of short on money and I really couldn't afford buying myself something at this point.

Doris—Right. You're the one who needs to fill in those lost cigarette strokes, Brian. And they will have to be meaningful to you or you won't give up the smoking.

BRIAN—I see that.

Doris—I'd like to comment further on one thing I mentioned earlier. When you suggested shopping, you were in your Parent ego state, Kate. You continued to work with Brian in your Parent by telling him you would check with him in two weeks. If Brian's Adult was not in on the act, his Child *just might* decide to rebel next week against Mommy and not keep his contract.

KATE—[Laughter] Yeah, I see that, Doris. You wouldn't do that, would you, Brian?

BRIAN—[Laughter] Not me.

Doris—We all know that smoking is a hard thing to give up. I would guess that since Brian made the contract with

Kate's Parent he won't keep it. I think it would be a good idea, Brian, if you worked on that issue more. What do you think?

BRIAN—I agree. I feel pretty scared that I won't keep it.

Doris—What do you want to do about that Brian?

BRIAN—I would like to work on it more.

Doris—How would you like to do that?

BRIAN—I know that I will not keep the contract now. I would like to think about it and come in later.

Doris—Okay. I think that's a good idea to give yourself time to think. Okay, Kate, tell us what you liked about your therapy.

KATE—I liked that I asked what the advantages were in giving up smoking. Also, I felt so much calmer doing therapy this time.

Doris—How many times have you been a therapist in here, Kate?

KATE—Three times. I'm doing good. Three times in six weeks.

Doris—Right. Okay. How about giving each other feedback?

KATE—I felt closest to you, Brian, when you said you wanted to give up cigarette smoking. I also felt close, and this might sound crazy, but I felt close when I was suggesting you go shopping for yourself. Like I wanted to take care of you.

Doris—When you were a child, did you get a lot of attention and good strokes for taking care of people?

KATE—Yes. I practically raised my younger sister. Oh, okay . . . I see. I feel good when I'm taking care of people because that's what good little girls do.

Doris—Yes. Lots of therapists were stroked as children for taking care of other people. Many times that's what prompts their being a therapist. Some taking care of other people is important, but if you are *always* taking care of your fellow travelers, they will never leave you to take care of themselves.

Lucy—That's really good information, Doris.

Doris—Thanks.

Brian—All right. I'll give my feedback now. The time I felt closest to you, Kate, was when you were talking about smokes actually being strokes. The time I felt farthest away was when you suggested that I buy myself some new clothes.

Kate—I understand that.

Later That Same Day

Brian—I would like to come back in now and deal with the issue of making a contract about smoking.

Doris—Who do you want to be your therapist?

Brian—I would like to work with you or Carla.

Doris—You need to be specific.

Brian—I'll work with you, Doris.

Doris—All right. What do you want to do, Brian?

Brian—I thought about the information. I know that I made the contract to please my Parent and Kate's Parent. What I would like to do is think about it and come back next week and work some more on this issue, but I was scared that everyone would be mad at me if I waited.

Doris—The contract is for you, Brian, not for us. It's okay to do what you need to do for yourself.

Brian—Thanks, Doris; I needed to hear that. Okay, I will come back next week and work on this again.

In the next transcript you will see a training session for advanced therapists. All of these therapists are actually doing therapy in the community. They have come to the training sessions either to learn more about group process, Transactional

Analysis, or Gestalt Therapy. I use the same structure for feedback with these therapists as I do with the beginning therapists.

The advanced therapists also work on their own issues. At first it may seem scary that people who are actually therapists in the community still have problems. The reality of it is that everyone has problems—therapists, too. When the advanced therapists work on their problems, they are often in their Child ego state just as anyone else. What I stress with the therapists is that they know their problem areas and that they make sure they separate *their* issues from those of their fellow travelers.

A TRAINING SESSION
FOR ADVANCED THERAPISTS

Doris—Morning everyone.

GROUP—Hi . . . Hi.

Doris—Any old business?

MARIE—No, but I have a question, Doris. How much should we know about drugs?

Doris—Well, let's see. You will need to know the major tranquilizers like Thorazine and Mellaril, the anti-anxiety drugs like Librium and Valium. Also, know the anti-depressants, Elavil, Triavil, and all the hallucinogens, like L.S.D., S.T.P., and marijuana and also the various barbiturates.

And speaking of knowing your drugs . . . a couple of months ago a woman came in to get some training in group process and was staying the week at our house. One night she complained about cramps and asked if I had any Donnatol. I said, "Yes," and proceeded to give her a tablet. Five hours later, I gave her another one. Well, the following morning as I was brushing my teeth, there was this bottle of pills . . . except to my horror . . .the pills weren't Donnatol at all . . . the pills were worm pills!!!

GROUP—[Roars of laughter.]

Doris—Last fall the second grade at school had an epidemic of

worms and so our family had to take worm pills.
[Laughter.] I suggest you know your drugs.

GROUP—[More laughter.]

Doris—Okay. Enough of this. Any other unfinished business?

GROUP—[Laughter] No . . . No.

Doris—All right. Who would like to be therapist?

TED—I would. Who would like to work?

RHONDA—I would. The issue I want to talk about is my legal
rights as a married woman. The problem is that Bruce, my
husband, and I see things differently. Things like inheri-
tance rights, estate planning. If something would happen
to Bruce, I don't know what the children or I would do.
I'm scared. Bruce doesn't like to talk about wills or death.
Yet I feel it's something that we have to talk about. If I
would die first, there wouldn't be a problem. I don't own
anything in my own right. If something would happen to
Bruce, then I would have to deal with certain things. What
would I do with Bruce's business? Where are our insurance policies? A lot of issues like this. In the past when I
have brought this issue up, Bruce's response has been,
"Everything is in your name, therefore there's nothing for
you to worry about." Almost like, "I love you, trust me,
everything is yours." But that's not the point. I know
everything is signed in my name. The point is, if I inherited
the business, I wouldn't know how to liquidate it. I don't
know who to go see. I don't know where insurance policies
are.

TED—[Therapist] Rhonda, I'm wondering what it is that you
want.

RHONDA—Um, well . . . uh . . . a couple of weeks ago I listened to
a woman lawyer speak on the subject and I really got fired
up. So once again, I brought the subject up with Bruce.
Again he seemed to laugh it off. I really got angry. I told
him that I would like to set up a date to go see an attorney.
He first said that he didn't want to talk about it, but then
he came around and said, "Okay, let me think about it." A

week went by and I asked him where he was with it. I said that I would like to set up an appointment at the end of December with an attorney. We have no will, and this really bothers me.

TED—[Therapist] What happened when you told Bruce what you wanted to do?

RHONDA—Well, it isn't the end of December yet.

Doris—All right, let's stop. Ted, let's have a conference before you go on.

TED—Okay.

RHONDA—Okay.

Doris—Ted, you asked a good question, "What is it that you want?" And what Rhonda did with the question was to give you lots of information, but not answer the question. So at this time, I'm not sure if it is her husband that she needs to deal with, or if it's the Parent in her head that says it is the man in the family that has the right to make the decisions. Or does Rhonda need to talk to a lawyer? Rhonda is not being clear with you about what she needs or wants to do.

TED—Okay, so I'll ask Rhonda what she wants to do.

Doris—Fine.

TED—[Therapist] Okay, Rhonda, I want to know what you want to do, specifically.

RHONDA—Well, Bruce doesn't think we really need to see a lawyer, but I do.

TED—[Therapist] What is Bruce's objection to a lawyer?

Doris—Okay. Let's stop. You just bought into a con, Ted. Your question, "What do you want to do?" never got answered. What do you want to do as the therapist?

TED—I would like to stop because I don't think I'm getting anywhere today, but I do want to do therapy again. However, I would like to say one more thing. And . . .um . . . you need to get clear, Rhonda, about what you want. [said angrily].

Doris—Okay, Ted. When I asked you what you wanted to do, you made a decision not to continue working with Rhonda. Then you gave her feedback about being unclear and you sound angry. So who are you angry with?

TED—I'm angry with you, Doris, because you stopped me, and I'm angry at Rhonda for being so fuzzy.

Doris—Well, I did stop you because I saw you allowing Rhonda to be unclear.

TED—You're right. I did bad therapy today.

Doris—Listen, it's important that you don't kick yourself. You did a lot of good things. Are you ready to hear about them or do you want to continue with the internal critical stuff and be a Victim?

TED—I want to hear the good stuff. [laughter].

Doris—Okay, Ted, what I liked was the way you let Rhonda run out her issue in the beginning, and the question you asked about what it was that she wanted. Your voice was clear. Also, you didn't stay in the Victim position. Everybody makes mistakes when they do therapy. Everyone is not so good about taking responsibility for their mistakes.

TED—Thanks, I feel better.

Doris—I'd like you to say what you liked about your therapy.

TED—I liked that I asked Rhonda what it was that she wanted.

Doris—Now, would you both give each other feedback?

TED—Rhonda, I felt closest to you when you started talking about your problem. I felt farthest away when you weren't clear as to what you wanted to work on.

RHONDA—And I felt closest to you at the beginning. I could see you were listening. I felt farthest away when you asked what I wanted to work on.

BURT—Hmm . . . That's interesting, Rhonda, that you felt close when Ted listened but not when he wanted you to do something about solving the problem.

RHONDA—I can see that. I've never thought about that.

Doris—Good feedback, Burt. Might be good for you to think about that, Rhonda.

RHONDA—Yeah.

Doris—Okay, who wants to be therapist?

LIDDY—I'll be therapist.

MARIE—I'll work. And boy, do I need to. Frank and I just returned from visiting my folks in New York for two weeks, and I have never been so miserable. My mother and I fought like cats and dogs. There wasn't anything I said that pleased her. I told her that Frank and I had just moved into bigger offices and instead of her being glad, she told me I should be feeling scared because of the economic situation. And didn't I know any better? Just because I was a therapist with a good position didn't imply I was a good money manager. That's what she told me!

LIDDY—[Therapist] What do you want from your mother?

MARIE—[Starting to cry] I want her to love me. To tell me she's so proud of me. To tell me I've been a good daughter. But . . . [crying] I know she won't. She hasn't for twenty-nine years. Why should she now? I'm the one that needs to change.

LIDDY—[Therapist] Change in what way?

MARIE—I need to stop hoping that she will see the light. I need to stop *caring* that she will come through. I know Frank loves me. The kids love me. I'm good at what I do . . . so why do I keep torturing myself? Why do I keep waiting for her to say I'm a good girl?

LIDDY—[Therapist] Why do you keep waiting?

MARIE—Maybe . . . maybe because she has never said it. How do I convince myself that I don't *need* my mother's approval?

LIDDY—[Therapist] Well, instead of trying to convince yourself that you don't need her approval, how about telling me how you would be different if she gave her approval . . . if she said, "You are a good daughter, Marie."

MARIE—How would I be different? Umm . . . well . . . uh . . . I *wouldn't* be different. I'd still be me. [Laughter] I might feel a little better, but I'd still be me.

LIDDY—[Therapist] And how will you be if you never get her approval?

MARIE—A little sad . . . but not so sad. I'll still be me. I guess I really don't need her approval. I know what I've done for me.

LIDDY—[Therapist] You *guess* you don't need her approval?

MARIE—I mean, I don't *need* her approval to be happy. Okay, I'm finished. Thanks, Liddy. You were great!

LIDDY—And you were easy to work with, Marie.

Doris—Good job! You stayed with Marie all the way. Your therapy really flowed. I especially was impressed with the question about how Marie would be different if she did get her mother's approval.

LIDDY—And what I liked about my therapy was my own calmness and the permission I gave Marie to have her feelings. I didn't try to hurry her through them.

EMILY—You did a fine job, Liddy.

BURT—Really good work, Liddy.

LIDDY—Gee thanks. My day is made! Okay, Marie, I felt closest to you, well, I felt close most of the time. I felt farthest away when you wanted to convince yourself that you needed your mother's approval.

MARIE—I felt closest to you when you asked me how I would be if my mother didn't approve and farthest away when you asked me why I kept waiting for her approval.

Doris—Okay. Let's take a break.

❖❖❖❖❖❖❖❖❖❖❖❖❖❖❖❖❖❖❖❖❖❖❖

This last transcript is a segment of a training session where Ron, one of the trainees, announces that he has made arrangements to teach a TA course at one of the local universities.

Though Ron had a Ph.D. in counseling, he was not trained in TA. Not only that, but he had often infuriated the group by playing Stupid about TA. The group, which was usually supportive and stroking when others had good news to share, reacted negatively to Ron's news. He was given much information as to why he should not teach the course.

WHAT'S ALL THE HOOPLA ABOUT?

Ron—I want to share something with the group. I'm going to be offering an introductory course in TA through the extension division of the university starting in two weeks. It will be a nine week course and people will get two hours of credit.

Doris—Have you ever taken a basic course in TA, Ron?

Ron—No.

Doris—And how long have you been in this group?

Ron—Two months.

Doris—Well, I don't think you're qualified to offer such a course.

Carla—I don't either, and I feel angry that you're doing it.

Doris—I don't like it when people in the community represent themselves as being able to teach TA when they are not familiar with the material.

Ron—I was aware that you would disapprove of my teaching.

Doris—Because?

Ron—Because of what you just said. I haven't had much training. But a basic course . . .

Doris—It's the principle of the thing, Ron. It would be like me teaching a class in Physics with two months of Physics. You're not qualified. What happened with Tom Harris' book, *I'm Okay You're Okay*, is that a lot of people read his book and then went out and taught TA—or claimed to be a TA therapist. This gives TA a bad name.

RON—I hear your concern.

Doris—I want you to hear my anger, too. What I'm also angry about is how you discount reality. You assume that you're qualified to teach something that you're really not qualified to teach. And I feel, whether it would be you or anybody else, I feel angry enough to write to the university and tell them that I think it's inappropriate that you're teaching. I think it's a shame.

RON—Okay, I hear that you two guys think I'm not qualified. And you have an idea about, in your head, as to what qualifications are necessary before a person teaches a TA course. And I disagree with that.

Doris—There are standards set by the national organization. So if you persist and refuse to cancel the course, I will call the university and state that I do not think you are qualified to teach. I think that you're jumping on the TA bandwagon because right now it's popular, and I also know that you could offer other courses. You are very qualified to teach Communication Theory.

DALE—You know, Ron, what a way for you to mess up. That's been one of your issues in here—how you take on something you shouldn't and then make a mess of it.

RON—Well, teaching TA should be easy.

DALE—I'm mad at you for saying that. You know TA is not easy. We work hard in here and then you come along and say how easy it is.

EMMA—I feel sad because if you were teaching something like Communication Theory we could feel good about you. You'd be getting lots of good strokes instead of everyone being mad at you.

SAL—Also, I think that decision was a set-up to put Carla, Doris, and the group in their disapproving Parents, then you can be a Victim.

RON—I don't agree. TA is no big deal.

Carla—I agree with Doris. I think you're jumping on the bandwagon and you don't even know what the band's playing, let alone how to play an instrument. I'm really mad.

RON—Well, I don't see myself as riding as the coattails of TA or jumping on the bandwagon.

Doris—Okay. I would like you to think about what you are going to do. If you choose to go ahead with your plans, I will take action. And I want to know by Thursday what you're going to do.

RON—Okay. I'll let you know.

The Training Session the Following Week

RON—I want to announce that during the week I talked with Doris and with the Director of the Extension Division at the university and I have decided to drop the course.

Doris—I would like to know why you made that decision, Ron. I know last week that we really confronted you about your teaching that course, and you were really fighting.

RON—Well, I have to say I was furious with this group. I was also scared, Doris. Finally, I sat myself down and went over what everyone had said by doing the "empty chair." I have to admit I woke myself up when I was responding to myself. Then I knew you were right.

Doris—Tell us three reasons why you made the decision.

RON—All right. First I made the decision because I know I don't know enough about TA and I would mess up. Secondly, I want to be close to people in here and I was setting it up that people would be angry and withdraw from me. Third, I decided to accept a job I'd been offered at another school where I'd be working in my field. I also must say that knowing that Doris would do something spurred me on. I didn't want her to be telling the director that I shouldn't be teaching the course.

GROUP—Good . . . I'm glad . . . . Me, too.

SHERI—That must have been very hard for you to do, Ron.

RON—You're right. I also want to say that I felt very bad about the way I set myself up last week and also the way I set the group up. I apologize.

Doris—Good. I like the way you worked this through outside of group. Now, how about getting support from the people in here. People recognize how tough it was to cancel the course, Ron.

RON—Right. Okay.

This last transcript was included in order to help increase your awareness that some people teach therapeutic concepts when they are not qualified. Worse yet, some people actually hang up shingles and do therapy when they are not qualified. Therapy, more than other fields, has its charlatans. This is important to keep in mind if you decide to get training as a therapist, or if you decide to go into a therapy group. As I stated before, the first thing you should do is to find a therapist who has been trained and supervised to do group therapy. A particular degree is no assurance that a person has received training and supervision or is a good therapist.

❖❖❖❖❖❖❖❖❖❖❖❖❖❖❖❖❖❖❖❖❖❖❖❖

In this book I have included transcripts of people who succeeded in making new decisions and changes in their lives, as well as transcripts of people who would not take the risk to change. Even though one may be dissatisfied with one's life, change can be frightening, because when one gives up a certain form of behavior there is often the fear that there will be nothing to take its place. Since people fear the unknown, they often hold onto old patterns of behavior that are familiar and seem safer. Because of this fear, people require a potent therapist who can give a great deal of *information*, *protection*, *permission*, *reassurance*, and *stroking*.

NOTES

1. Aaron Wolfe Schiff and Jacqui Lee Schiff, "Passivity," *Transactional Analysis Journal*, I, 1 (1971), pages 71 – 78.

2. Vic Green, former member of the Asklepieion Foundation, Carbondale, Illinois.

3. Eric Berne, *Transactional Analysis in Psychotherapy* (New York: Grove Press, 1961), pages 17 – 43.

4. Eric Berne, *The Structure and Dynamics of Organizations and Groups* (Philadelphia: J. B. Lippincott, 1963), page 157.

5. Eric Berne, *Games People Play* (New York: Grove Press, 1964), pages 29 – 64.

6. *Ibid.*, page 33.

7. Eric Berne, *What Do You Say After You Say Hello?* (New York: Grove Press, 1972), page 24.

8. Eric Berne, *Games People Play*, pages 48 – 64.

9. Stephen B. Karpman, "Fairy Tales and Script Drama Analysis," *Transactional Analysis Bulletin*, VII, No. 26 (April, 1968), pages 39 – 43.

10. David Kupfer and Morris Haimowitz, "Therapeutic Interventions—Part I, Rubberbands Now," *Transactional Analysis Journal* (April, 1971) 1:1, pages 10 – 16.

11. Eric Berne, *Games People Play*, pages 84 – 86.

12. *Ibid.*, pages 115 – 122.

13. Muriel James and Dorothy Jongeward, *Born To Win* (California: Addison-Wesley Publishing, 1971), page 168.

14. Stanley Woollams, M.D., Michael Brown, Ph.D., Kristyn Huige, M.A., *Transactional Analysis in Brief* (Huron Valley Institute: 1974), page 38.

15. Natalie and Morris Haimowitz, "Introduction to Transactional Analysis," *Human Development*, ed. Morris and Natalie Haimowitz (New York: Thomas Y. Crowell, 1973), page 349.

16. Stanley Woollams, M.D., Michael Brown, Ph.D., Kristyn Huige, M.A., *Transactional Analysis in Brief*, page 31.

17. Eric Berne, *Games People Play*, pages 83 – 84.

18. *Ibid.*, pages 123 – 124.

19. Eric Berne, *What Do You Say After You Say Hello?*, pages 335 – 337.

20. Robert Zechnich, "Social Rapo—Description and Cure," *Transactional Analysis Journal*. III (October, 1973), pages 18 – 21.

21. Aaron and Jacqui Schiff, "Passivity," *Transactional Analysis Journal*, pages 71 – 78.

22. Eric Berne, *Games People Play*, pages 91 – 94.

23. *Ibid.*, pages 159 – 162.

24. *Ibid.*, pages 130 – 131.

So you found *Group Therapy - Who Needs It* interesting and helpful. Doris also believes that people want and need more information in the areas of dating, sexual compatibility, choosing a mate, parenting skills, assertiveness training, management training, and other areas of interpersonal relationships.

If you, or a friend, would like to receive periodic information about books and programs regarding these topics of interest, Doris will be happy to send information in these areas as it becomes available.

Please send your name and permanent mailing address to:

Doris Wild Helmering
P.O. Box 24235
St. Louis, Missouri 63130

BOOKS OF RELATED INTEREST

A transactional analysis of game-playing in the classroom, Ken Ernst's GAMES STUDENTS PLAY provides insight and guidance to anyone who interacts with children or young adults. 128 pages, soft cover, $4.50; hard cover, $7.95

Family therapist Kathryn Hallett's A GUIDE FOR SINGLE PARENTS shows how, by means of Transactional Analysis, personal loss such as divorce, separation, desertion or death can provide growth rather than paralysis and despair. 128 pages, soft cover, $3.95

From the author of GAMES STUDENTS PLAY, PRE–SCRIPTION: A TA LOOK AT CHILD DEVELOPMENT by Ken Ernst provides ways to deal with harmful "scripts" before they develop in children. 128 pages, soft cover, $4.50

In THE INWARD JOURNEY, art therapist Margaret Frings Keyes integrates Gestalt techniques with Transactional Analysis and Jungian thought in a rich and illuminating guide for the lay reader to the use of art as therapy. 128 pages, soft cover, $4.95

CELESTIAL ARTS
Millbrae, California